Practical Study Skills
for Nurses

Practical Study Skills for Nurses

JOE WINTERS

MN RGN RMN DipN (Lond)
Clinical Nurse Specialist – Greater Glasgow Community and
Mental Health Services NHS Trust

Scutari Press · London

© Scutari Press 1995

A division of Scutari Projects Ltd, the publishing company of the Royal College of Nursing.

First published 1995

British Library Cataloguing in Publication Data
Winters, Joe
    Practical Study Skills for Nurses
    I. Title
    610.7307

ISBN 1–873853–15–7

Typeset by J&L Composition Ltd, Filey, North Yorkshire
Printed and bound in Great Britain Redwood Books, Trowbridge, Wiltshire.

Contents

For my mother, Anne, and in memory of my father, Martin

Preface

While I will always consider myself a learner, I have never felt a deep and abiding drive to excel at my studies for their own sake. I would much rather learn something in order to use it in a practical way. I have tried to write this book to reflect that point of view, offering advice, guidance and instruction in as practical a manner as I can manage on a subject that I believe will be a crucial factor in the future of nursing in this country.

The education of nurses, whether before or after Registration, is becoming increasingly academically inclined as time passes – which is how it *should* be. If we are to consolidate, increase and diversify our contributions to modern health care, we need to be competent and capable learners. However, the skills we require in order to achieve these benefits are not 'academic' skills in the sense of being solely concerned with intellectual affairs, divorced from our experiences of practical matters. Instead, these skills must be tools with which we can build for ourselves an appropriate and expanding knowledge base upon which we practise the profession.

The personal educational development of each and every one of us lies at the heart of the development of nursing, because it is what *we* do as individuals that determines the level and quality of nursing care. On that basis, the suggestions and recommendations I make in this book about studying and learning are made with practical purposes in mind. I hope you find them useful.

JW

Acknowledgements

I am grateful to John Naish who, while Viewpoint Editor at *Nursing Standard*, recommended that I take the idea for this book to Jim McCarthy, Commissioning Editor at Scutari Press. Jim's patient support and courteous suggestions made the whole thing painless.

I also want to thank my family – Geraldine, Martin, Laura and Lynne, for their absence of doubt about my authorship, and lack of recrimination for the reduction of my share of the housework.

Lastly, I want my friend and fellow-learner Brian McMahon to know that it was his constant belief in me, which went beyond reason or proof, that convinced me I could do this.

1 Basic equipment

WANTING TO LEARN, WANTING TO REMEMBER

All of us have the ability to learn: to take in information and make use of it. The process of learning, of handling information, is what makes us able to deal with the world, and no matter what you may think of yourself, you're a capable learner. You can speak, read and write, which proves you can master complex tasks in learning. What you do with those skills now is entirely dependent upon what you *choose* to do with them.

This matter of choosing to apply yourself to learning is often overlooked, especially so in the light of many people's experience of their schooldays, when learning was often closely associated with the requirement to do as you were told. For many of us, whether we're fresh from school or not, learning was influenced by obedience, and that obedience was used to impose certain types of behaviour, such as doing homework and taking examinations. But in the sense of being a lifelong reason for learning, obedience falls a long way short of meeting the needs of the adult learner. Moreover, for some adults, the memories they have of learning in school can underpin a reluctance to learn in later life; we might suggest that some of us have almost been conditioned to find learning difficult because of past experiences. Most people have anecdotes to tell from their childhood about bad-tempered teachers who were continually bullying and berating their students. Whether these are 'true' or not doesn't matter – it can be very difficult to come out of traditional schooling with a positive frame of mind about learning, to be enthusiastic about the acquisition and use of information. It is important to recognise, too, that this negative outlook can be linked in us with the belief that we are 'poor' learners, that we aren't as smart or as capable as other people.

These two perceptions – a dislike of learning and a low intellectual self-esteem – can combine so strongly and unwittingly in us that they become the foundations of a self-fulfilling prophecy: we're convinced that we can't learn, and the result is that we don't.

However, none of that is true for any of us. We are able to learn, to acquire and use knowledge; and while bad learning experiences in the past are unfortunate, and might account for a personal history of poor educational performance at some stage in our lives, each of us has the right to believe that no part of the learning process is beyond our ability. All that's required of us is the decision to make a commitment to learning, and the willingness to make the necessary effort.

Once that decision is consciously taken, with the realisation of all that it implies, any act of learning becomes a matter of self-government, of directing yourself and your ability towards doing what you need to do in order to learn.

There are three personal qualities which will underpin any learning experience, each of which can be 'practised' so that they work to your benefit – Attitude, Motivation and Perseverance.

ATTITUDE

What is your attitude to learning, to studying? If you've never considered this before, do it now. You might find that evidence for your attitude is best described in statements you've made in the past about events that have to do with learning. If these statements are consistently positive, all well and good. However, many of us have a range of negative comments that we use whenever the subject of learning comes up – for example, 'I'm hopeless at Exams, can't remember a thing', 'I was never any good at Maths, numbers are a nightmare', 'Chemistry was beyond me', or even 'I slept through History classes, they were so boring'. When we use remarks like these then, whatever else they might be, they are statements about who we think we are, in terms of what we believe we are unable to do. These negative statements are usually based on events in our lives that happened years before. No matter that our personal circumstances might have radically changed since then, or even that more positive learning experiences have occurred in the interim, we very often become caught in the trap of seeing ourselves as being somehow incapable of learning well.

Even if these statements were ever 'true', they are less important in themselves than in how their repetition brings you to believe in them, and how that belief might influence your behaviour.

The point is that you can choose whether to see yourself as a good and capable learner, or not. It all depends on your attitude to yourself and your learning. The basic premise to adopting a positive attitude is that the course of education you're following is worthwhile and you're going to make the most of it. That sounds simple, but if you're harbouring negative beliefs about your ability to learn, the second part can be difficult to accept. The easiest way to overcome these counter-productive ideas is to behave as though they didn't exist, to perceive them as useless and out-dated personal notions that have no part in your life. Regardless of how these beliefs came about, you can choose to ignore them. When you do so you can begin to create new circumstances, new events, that will foster in you a positive attitude to learning.

An attitude is a frame of mind, and you can choose to change your mind. You can alter your beliefs, change your outlook and adopt a positive stance. All it takes is a decision not to let yourself be hampered by the past.

MOTIVATION

Your motivation to learn, just like your attitude, can be created by you as an act of will. Again, the starting point is to 'unlearn' what you may have believed in the past, especially if you considered motivation to study as being something you never possessed.

The most important thing to get straight in your mind is that while there might be countless external events that can stimulate your motivation, such as examinations, motivation itself is a personal property. Obviously the two are linked, but if you have no clear motivation to learn, external prompts will fail in helping you to deal with your learning. In this context, we can view motivation as 'the desire to do', where that 'doing' is concerned with each and every aspect of any learning experience.

The seeds of your own motivation can be very personal, but whatever they are you have to recognise them and make them strong, because they are important to you. Motivation to learn might spring from a desire to succeed in a course and secure employment afterwards. It might arise from a wish to excel, or from a determination to 'better' yourself. What-ever your motivation is, whatever causes you to learn, should be identi-fied and worked on, developed clearly and used as a source of inspiration and energy.

For most of us learning is very rarely seen as a goal in itself; we can recognise and value learning, but we usually make the effort that learning requires when we set our sights on something that learning can bring us. You might find it helpful to consider closely just why you're undertaking a learning experience, and try writing your reasons down on paper. Explore these reasons fully in an attempt to define the gains a successful effort will produce for you. When you've arrived at a complete list, however short or long it might be, write each of them out in as positive a way as you can. For instance, if completing a course is important to your job prospects and you've written 'If I fail this course I'll be unemployed', change it to, for example, 'When I pass this course a whole career will open up for me'.

Remind yourself regularly of these reasons for success, read them over and think about them. Most importantly, believe that you can make them happen. If you find this difficult at first, that nagging thoughts of self-doubt make the whole idea of your success seem foolish, don't give up. Keep practising, keep behaving as though you were convinced of your eventual success, because in that behaviour you will be demonstrating to yourself that you are willing to do the things necessary to succeed. You will be exercising, and proving, your motivation.

The motivation to learn comes in many different guises. Whatever works for you, find it and cultivate it; it's an essential part of the learning process.

PERSEVERANCE

Positive attitudes and high levels of motivation are all very well, but what happens if these slide away and you just run out of steam? When, no matter what the current demands on you are, all you want to do is close the books and give up? This can happen when you're under a lot of stress, perhaps just before exams, but it can also occur (and more insidiously) when you're passing through some stage in your course when the only 'threats' to you as a learner are comfortably far off. The only thing you can do is the most obvious one: just stick with it and persevere.

This is much easier said than done but it is possible, and the best way to achieve it is to continue to do those things required of you as a learner as though you were still in a positive frame of mind: maintain your usual study habits. No matter how you feel about it, keep to the routines and schedules you set yourself for getting through your course – attend your classes and listen, complete assignments on time, stay in touch with your learning and never lose sight of what you want to achieve by it.

That last point is very important when you find yourself in the doldrums. Even if, deep down, you see persevering at your studies to be no more than just 'going through the motions', you can still appreciate that the effort is worthwhile: hold on to that and do what needs to be done.

I've chosen to spend time on covering some of the personal attributes that can influence learning because it's important for us to recognise that what we gain from any learning experience is in proportion to the efforts we choose to make. In considering this notion of 'effort', we have to accept that it can be heavily coloured by further personal perspectives, and the most troublesome of these can be self-delusion and intellectual inertia.

SELF-DELUSION

In your learning, you cannot afford to be anything less than brutally honest with yourself. You must be certain that you come to grips with the learning required of you, and you will make no appreciable moves towards that state unless and until you make a complete appraisal of yourself as a motivated individual who has consciously chosen to learn. That might sound obvious, or unpalatably didactic; but if you reflect on it, you might find that you have undergone past learning experiences because you had to, because circumstances required or forced you to – in which case, your behaviour as a learner might be seen as being 'controlled' by outside events. You're in a different situation now, and you have to make a measured and reasonable consideration of what you're bringing to your present experience. You have to 'take stock' of yourself, and be in no doubt that you alone are responsible for your learning.

It can be seductively easy as a learner to 'assign responsibility' for success or failure to someone or something else, usually perceived by us as being completely outside our ability to control. In this way, we think we will succeed if only we are taught by this teacher instead of that one, if the exams we take are as easy this year as they were last year, and we will fail because the course never prepared us properly and anyway, everybody knows that the examiners have been instructed to fail a third of the class – it keeps up standards.

None of this is true, and the quicker we come to understanding that the quality and quantity of our learning is directly under our personal control then the easier it becomes to assume responsibility for that learning and to use it for our own benefit. Any other perception is a snare and a delusion.

INTELLECTUAL INERTIA

The knowledge that learning takes effort can inhibit the best of us from making any effort at all. Not that we put it to ourselves in quite that way; we're happier to tell each other that some subjects are more interesting than others and if we could just get through the course studying only our favourite subjects then there would be no problem.

However, for most of us learning isn't an intellectual game, an interesting hobby with which to while away the hours. We have to do what's required to learn, and that 'doing' always requires effort. The secret to making that effort lies in the justifications that you find for yourself in expending energy on learning.

You know this already: learning about subjects which interest you can seem almost effortless; learning about subjects which you believe are difficult or boring appears to use up vast amounts of energy very rapidly indeed. In reality, the effort you can make for both situations is the same; the only difference lies in the 'learning momentum' you bring to the task. That momentum, that energy, is under your control, factored and fed by the personal justifications you make for learning – 'I like this, I don't like that', 'This is interesting, that is tedious in the extreme' or, most influential of all, 'I don't really need to know this'. By the adroit use of personal likes and dislikes, it is entirely possible for a learner to carve up a curriculum into 'easy/hard, interesting/boring, important/pointless' lists of subjects just by reading the syllabus on the first day of a course, and thereafter to become intellectually inert when presented with any material that doesn't somehow suit them.

It doesn't have to be this way; successful efforts in learning can be made if they are underpinned by the decision to go ahead and make the effort in the first place. Once that decision is made, then learning can begin and can be built upon. There is no doubt that some areas of knowledge are more complex, more extensive than others, and some learning experiences prove more enjoyable than others. Subjects and circumstances differ, but you can still control how you will perceive them, how you will deal with them, how you will learn.

To sum up this section, we can note that your personal attributes as an individual will greatly influence your performance as a learner and that learning isn't some quirky ability that might or might not present itself when called upon: it's something you can do, something you're good at, a personal capacity which you can improve upon. The only insurmountable obstacles to your learning are those which you allow yourself to be convinced are real.

When it comes to the mechanics of learning, the simplest place to begin is with the skills of Attention and Concentration.

ATTENTION AND CONCENTRATION

No matter how smart you are, merely staying conscious on a course won't be enough. You're going to have to pay attention and you're going to have to concentrate. Since you're reading this, you can already do both; all you have to do now is practise them as skills.

Paying attention means putting a focus on your consciousness in literally 'attending' to what you're seeing and hearing. Being attentive is an activity which you can bolster by conscious choice.

Concentration is achieved by sustained attention, by choosing to retain the focus of that attention until you're ready to relinquish it.

These are plain statements, and if we all had the knack of producing a closely focused attention and then maintaining it *ad infinitum* no more would need to be said; being human, though, just about any stimulus can distract our attention and interfere with our concentration. The real knack to acquire is the ability to ignore distractions.

Distractions to learning come in many and varied guises, but they can be boiled down to just two categories – those that originate from outside us, and those that come from within. Leaving aside life-threatening situations and overwhelming needs to maintain bodily health and comfort, it doesn't matter from which vector the distraction comes; the only thing that counts is whether you will choose to pay any attention to it. That choice will be influenced by the strength of your intention to stay on the track of whatever it is you're being distracted from.

This intention must be prepared and strengthened as a stimulus to learn, to the point where it outweighs, in personal value to you, any other stimulus that will compete for your attention. You cannot prevent every distraction, but you can decide not to be distracted. Attention and concentration can be practised to the point where they become a habit of behaviour, when the intention to focus on what we're doing becomes strong and ingrained to the point of seeming automatic.

The actual process of learning involves higher functions of the brain, but for most learners the prime focus of concern in whether they learn or not revolves around their ability to remember. There are a number of theories as to how human memory works, but for our purposes here we can propose that no matter how it actually works, our ability to store information in the memory and retrieve it at will can always benefit from regular exercise. This exercise can take place in two steps – Repetition and Recall.

Repetition

The information you will be exposed to in your course will rarely be simple or striking enough for you to remember it easily and instantly. The likelihood is that most of your acquisition of material will come about by repeated exposure. Information has to be handled appropriately by your brain before it can be used consciously and at will. The simplest way to ensure that information is stored as an accessible memory is to give your brain a chance.

Get into the habit of going over material you want to learn more than just once. Accept that it may take a while to 'stick'. This is not simply a matter of doing things by rote – you're trying to *learn*, not just memorise. When you repeatedly handle the same information, you must continue to think about it, to actively consider its meaning.

There is no magic formula for repetition, no '10 repeats = 1 memory', but whenever you think about items of information they are handled that bit more, their 'shape' becomes more recognisable to you. Sooner or later, your willingness to process information will get results.

Recall

As we've noted, memory 'models' offer different explanations of how information is processed and stored in the human brain. No matter how this storage is achieved, you want to be sure you can retrieve information from that store when you need it; and this retrieval, or recall, can be practised.

On a regular basis, set aside time to just sit down and think about material you've learned. Conjure it up piece by piece and peruse it, consider it with care and ask yourself questions about it. Make your answers as detailed as possible. Say them out loud in complete sentences.

Especially with new information, make a conscious effort to discover and understand the links between bits of information. No body of knowledge is an unrelated jumble of 'facts and figures' – search for sequences and order, work out how one piece of information fits with another. It all helps you to create a better organisation of information in your memory, and improves your chances of having a ready access to material stored there.

The key point of course is practice, handling information again and again. Repeatedly sending information into your brain and then repeatedly recalling it is intended to bring the information to your attention and allow you to concentrate on it.

Repetition and Recall are very straightforward exercises in studying. There's no doubt that these 'rehearsals' of material can sometimes be tedious, but similarly there's no doubt they can pay dividends.

EXERCISING THE BRAIN

How much regular exercise does your brain get? Do you use it and stretch it, keep it fit and in good shape? Or does it normally just sit around, with no heavier demands made on it than to keep the rest of you ticking over? Is it running to seed, do you think? Are there times when it will barely start in the morning? Does it take you so far and then just run out of puff?

Here's a less than startling statement: we take our brains for granted. Some schools of thought hold that we generally use about 10 per cent of our brain's total capacity. Most of us would probably instinctively agree with that, and perhaps even privately admit that using as much as 10 per cent would be a gross exaggeration. For one reason or another, it can be very easy just to coast along and get by without drawing on the brainpower too much or too often.

Then we start an educational course, and find that getting the grey cells up to speed is a tortuous business; but what else can we expect? We couldn't walk into a gym and bench-press 300 lb of cast iron without practice, could we?

Why am I going on about this? For a very good reason – you might be facing the intellectual equivalent of that 300 lb weight right now and have already convinced yourself you couldn't shift it with a fork-lift truck, never mind your own muscles. Forget it, you might have told yourself, there's no way I can manage this.

Yes, you can. If you're willing to take the dust covers off the wetware and start using it, there's nothing to stop you. Nothing. All it takes is effort and exercise.

Oceans of Data in all Shapes and Sizes

Undertaking any educational course can be a daunting business. As one stage succeeds another great oceans of information are opened up, and all of it has somehow to be pumped in to your head. Where do you start? How will you cope?

Think

A very obvious beginning, but one that is so easy to overlook in the first fearful throes of a course. Think about it – nobody expects you to learn everything right away and all at once. Your course will be split into parts. The trick is to place yourself in each part *as it happens* and pay attention to what's happening *now*.

As soon as you acquire a course syllabus, go over it in detail. You'll find that it describes course material by Topic and by Time. That is, you'll be told *what* you must learn and *when* you are to learn it. Think this through, take your mind off the ocean of knowledge at the end of the course and fix it on reality – the drop by drop acquisition of learning is all that anyone is capable of and no one expects you to be any different. Don't be scared, be sensible. Think.

Think your way through each part of the course. As one learning experience looms up, is undergone and then replaced by another, where are you in all of this? Right in the middle, thinking; prepare yourself for learning, gear yourself up mentally to learn, limber up the brain to act and interact with information as it is presented in the course. Expect to think, look forward to it, give it all you've got.

Educational courses are constructed by human beings for other human beings, not by some hyperintelligent race from another galaxy. The same organ is used to create your course as the one you will use to deal with it. So think.

Plan

Don't let any part of your course take you by surprise. Never allow yourself to become disorientated as to where you are in the course. Plan your way through it, act before the event rather than react as it occurs. Be ready for each step and stage the syllabus lays out – acquire reading lists, timetables; plan your actions, take the initiative and make yourself ready.

Planning (it won't have escaped your notice) requires thought, in this case forethought: you're placing yourself squarely in the course and figuring out the moves you'll need to make next. Are there any books you must have, places you must be, work you should have done? See to it, and get ready.

Organise

For a learner, nothing is more important than thinking; but organisation comes close behind. Without good organisation, any course is liable to swamp you in a morass of disconnected data and work undone. If you've never been an organised type of person, now's the time to acquire the habit.

Consider your daily life and organise learning time within it. Classes and other formal learning exposures aside, where, when and how do you intend to study and learn? Will this take place regularly by sensible organisation or by chance? It's your life, how will you order it?

Without resorting to the excesses of obsession, don't let anything disturb your organisation. That includes any action on your part that might debilitate your good intentions. Organisation can become, perhaps not 'fun', but at least a way of building in a degree of acceptance that for some time to come, learning will be a part of your life.

Do

Think, Plan, Organise, Do. When thinking about your course prompts you to plan, and planning suggests organisation, then all that's left is to do whatever is necessary. To take action.

It can be very easy to fall into the habit as a learner of just accepting whatever experience comes your way. Being reactive to the demands of a course is one thing; taking a *proactive* attitude, creating and maintaining a level of activity that goes beyond being a passive responder, is another thing altogether.

Environment, Atmosphere and Distraction

Some people can study and learn just about anywhere, from standing upright in a subway train while being jostled by noisy crowds to propping their books against sauce bottles in staff cafeterias; these lucky individuals can switch on to learning no matter what's going on around them. However, for most of us, setting out to learn takes some preparation, and the ways in which we do this are often a reflection of our likes and dislikes, things that irk or please us and which we find it impossible to ignore.

When you have a lot of studying to do over a period of time, it pays to give a bit of thought to where, when and how it will be done. You might well have spent time getting yourself into the right frame of mind to study and learn, but what's next? Acquiring good study habits is what's next, and the first step towards this is to plan where it will take place.

Do you need a quiet place in order to study, or do you prefer a television or radio belting out background noise? Are you nearer the Holy Grail of learning on your own or in the company of others? Can you reject distractions or do they niggle away at you? Ask yourself these questions and others to find out exactly what you think. You need to discover just exactly *what suits you* so far as a study environment is concerned.

You might find, knowing yourself and your circumstances, that you can identify just one environment where you can study. You might be able to select several locations that are suitable. On the other hand, you might have to achieve a compromise between what you need and what's available. Whatever the outcome, consider it with care: it's true that a single place set aside just for study can be a great boon – as soon as you sit down in it you switch on the study habits; it's also true that habits can be broken when the environment in which they operate is changed. Getting into a groove for studying is good, being unable to wrench yourself out of a rut isn't. Similarly, using a series of locations for study can help to keep you fresh and prevent boredom – also, it might be an in-built excuse for wasting study time by choosing the one furthest away from where you are whenever you need to hit the books. Compromise arrangements can prove irksome in the extreme and very unsettling in the long run.

The whole point about finding a place to study is that, outside of educational institutions, the physical environments we spend our time in are given over to other purposes and used by other people. These two circumstances can combine to produce a fair degree of conflict for the individual intent on studying: sitting-rooms are comfortable and handy to use, but the patience of even the most supportive family members can wear very thin very quickly when the learner among them stacks their books on the sofa and insists on peace and quiet, for example. Essentially, you have to find a place in which you can 'be a student', a place in which you can gear yourself up for learning.

Once you've found that place, will you inhabit it on your own or share it with other learners? If studying alone suits you best then the choice is simple and 'intruders' can be politely dissuaded from disturbing you. However, there are some benefits to be had from setting up small study groups of like-minded people. The support that learners can give each other can be invaluable and opportunities for exchanging information should never go unconsidered. A good study group can knit itself together and generate a level of enthusiasm that might rarely be achieved by individual members working alone. Sometimes, everything clicks and group members develop a flair for particular material and teach it to the others. Studying in groups can provide very positive learning experiences.

However, it can also be disastrous. The group has to be well-chosen and people must be compatible. Unfortunately, compatibility is usually the only criterion used to determine the group membership, which, in one sense, is fair enough; if the people in the group don't like one another, there will either only ever be one meeting of the group or each meeting will be crammed with incidents you can all do without. 'Compatible', in this context, is more productive if seen at the level of 'genuinely co-operative' rather than 'bosom buddy'.

Choosing group members is another business all together. Whether you're doing the choosing or you've been asked by someone else to be in a study group, the same cautionary notes apply and can be summed up by two questions – *what* benefits are to be gained from participation and *who* gets these benefits?

The *what benefit* areas can be a little tricky to answer – if the purpose of having a study group hasn't been thoroughly considered by all concerned. Essentially the *promotion* of learning is what the group should be about; it should create and sustain a forum for study where like-minded people with the same purposes can work together towards common goals in learning. To acquire this benefit, you need group members for whom there are no obstacles to communication, who appreciate the need to co-operate with other people, and who are willing to collaborate with every other member of the group. The selection of people for the group must hinge on whether potential members have demonstrated these characteristics. That sounds a little cold, but it's necessary.

Who benefits is at one and the same time easy to answer and difficult to quantify. Everyone concerned should benefit. However, the degree of that benefit will depend heavily on the personal possession of a willingness to learn, to make the effort, to work at fulfilling the individual role that contributes to the purpose of the group.

Taking the *what* and *who* answers together, you can see that any study group worthy of the name can be wholly described as a *'learners' co-operative'* – where each member displays certain personality traits and social skills necessary for the group to function. Now, this idea might go a little beyond what you might have expected, but the whole business must be thought through with care – time on any course is finite, you can't commit yourself to any study group without first thinking what that commitment will require of you and without considering what effects it might have on your learning.

However, while benefits from membership of a study group might be less assured than they appear at first sight, they can be very substantial. You just have to be sure that you suit the group and the group suits you.

One last point on this subject which, mercenary and élitist though it might sound, needs to be said: if you happen to be a hard-working, knowledgeable, motivated self-starter perfectly capable of effective study on your own, think twice if demands are made on you to join a study group whose composition you suspect has the capacity to take a good deal more from you than it can possibly return. You might end up tutoring needy pals who see you as the *Reader's Digest* version of your course. I've said that teaching peers can be invaluable to you, and that's true. But you must never forget your own needs as a learner. There is a world of difference between teaching others in order to develop and deepen your own understanding of your learning, and spoonfeeding people who are perfectly willing to relinquish their personal responsibility for learning and shove it onto someone else at the first opportunity. I know this sounds harsh, but if you find yourself in this position, be wary, be polite, and above all – be elsewhere when the group meets.

2 Fundamental skills

ACTING AND INTERACTING/
VALUES AND BELIEFS

One of the most fundamental skills you bring to your learning is the ability to 'act' – to *do* something. It's obvious, but true, to say that learners are not empty vessels waiting to be filled to the brim with knowledge by teachers expert at cramming in every last drop of wisdom. Learning is not a passive experience. You have to play your part. You have to act and interact in order to learn, and do so with every piece of relevant information that comes your way. The acquisition of knowledge and the ability to use it appropriately are active processes. The source of energy for these activities must stem from you; you have to be prepared to *act*, to take responsibility for your actions, to take control and do whatever's required so that you will learn.

The driving principles for your activities as a learner come from the values and beliefs you hold about yourself and your learning, and all of these should be positive. If, right now, you know your course is worth pursuing and you know that you're ready, willing and able to undertake it, you're all set. If not, get it straight in your mind that you *must become involved* in what you're doing – this isn't a rehearsal for the course, this is it. Commit yourself to it and *participate*. Get your sleeves rolled up and get in there. Even if you still harbour any nagging doubts about whether you're up to the demands the course will make on you, make a conscious decision to face these demands and get ready to give everything your best shot. Don't wait for any Magic Moments of understanding to just happen, don't wait for some welling up of unshakeable confidence, don't hang around on the sidelines envying other people and their 'natural gifts' – get stuck in and be a learner. Make the investment of *doing*, of *acting*. It will pay dividends.

ACTIVE LISTENING, ACTIVE RESPONSE

The first active investment you can make is to listen. Connect the ears to the brain and let it act on what's coming in. Think about the information you receive through your ears and you're *listening* – registering data and acting upon it with your mind. Fail to think about it and you're *hearing* – the process by which sound waves are transmitted to the brain and die through neglect. If you're not a skilled listener, and it is most definitely a skill, you have to become one. Try practising – listen to what people say and paraphrase it in your head, think about it, ponder it, turn the information this way and that. Listening is the first and crucial step to extracting meaning from information you hear; give it a chance to come in – more, welcome it by preparing a place for it. Make yourself ready to listen.

The amount of time you'll spend sitting in front of lecturers will be considerable, so you should be ready to spend that time wisely and well, not least because actively listening is the essential precursor to making an active response.

When most lecturers say 'Are there any questions?', most learners look down and sit very still indeed. The result is that first-rate opportunities for learning go down the tubes for the lack of a little activity. If you've a lecturer before you to whom you've been listening, and something has been said that needs to be clarified, why wait until they've gone and then ask a classmate? Ask the person who said the thing in the first place. Make an active response – 'I'm not sure I understand your points about . . .' or 'Could you elaborate a little on . . .'. Why not? Consider this: if someone's there to teach and you're there to learn from them, what's so terrible about responding to what they're telling you? All right, social inhibition is what can make it terrible for some of us, the dread of speaking out and asking the dumbest question in the history of the world. Will that happen? No – the chances are that the majority of people sitting around us are desperate to ask the same question. Never be inhibited from making a response that is intended to assist you in your learning. Staying quiet might mean staying misinformed.

Essentially, your active responses to information coming in enable you to handle that information more, to pay attention to it for longer periods of time, to sort it and process it and make it a part of the whole of your knowledge and the way in which you understand and use it. In this sense, *all* information to which you have access deserves an active response. Any source of information can prompt you to think and consider; it's what you do with that prompt that's important. You can ignore it or use it as a stimulus for further learning. The choice is yours and it's an active choice.

The Automatic Learner

Staying conscious on a course and remaining aware of what's going on are not the same thing, although a lot of learners appear to believe they are. Turning up in the classroom at the right time with the right books in your bag falls a long way short of being all that's required of you. Each educational course has its own 'current', its own momentum, and sometimes it's very easy for learners just to go with the flow and become dragged along on the tide from the beginning to the end of their course, in which case, success or failure is a matter of chance.

This can be avoided. Taking responsibility for your own learning is the most fundamental step away from being an 'automatic' learner, and there is no better superstructure to build on this foundation than that of *critical thinking*.

The best way to define this critical thinking is first to make clear what it is not. It is *not* a frame of mind in which everything that comes to your attention is weighed in the balance and found 'good' or 'bad', and supported or denounced, retained or discarded depending on what you already 'know'. That is a recipe for disaster; you can't risk setting up some kind of dysfunctional 'filter' between yourself and the oceans of information that are out there. That information has to be allowed to come in and be acted upon in its 'natural' form – you can't afford to let it go by without comment, even if it is suitably clothed in your own opinions.

Critical thinking is a term that might be summed up as our refusal to suspend disbelief – our intention to subject all information to a scrutiny designed to search out and consider its meaning.

In this sense, critical thinking can be developed as a skill from the decision to actively 'question' information, to consider it with care and to never let any of it simply be accepted as 'truth'. It might be 'truth', or at least a hard-won, reasonably realistic and acceptable facsimile thereof – but until *you* have personally appraised it, it's just another item in a stream of data. It is the willingness to question, to appraise information, that feeds a conscious awareness in us as learners. Further, sometimes painfully acquired though it may be, the skill of critical thinking serves a great purpose in underwriting a lifelong ability to keep learning. It stops us from getting stale and it drives us to develop the other dimensions of a questioning outlook – analysis and evaluation.

Analysis and Evaluation

Any information you have access to in learning has to be analysed; it has to be dissected and examined before you 'know' it and can make use of it.

That's plain enough. What isn't so obvious is that analysis takes time, and can't be hurried – not if you want to learn and understand.

Spending time on analysing information is never wasted; at the very least you'll be exercising your skills in attention and concentration. More than that, though, you will be handling the material, learning what it has to teach you by taking it to bits, handling it and seeing how it all fits together. Remember that learning involves activity, your activity, and count analysis as an essential component of necessary learning 'behaviour'. Analysing information is like chewing your food properly. It helps you to reduce material to a form in which it can be better digested.

From analysis comes evaluation – which, as the word suggests, is the mechanism whereby you assign 'values' to information. In this context, these 'values' are directly related to the meanings which any information might have for you, where these 'meanings' deal not only with the ideas they represent, but also with their capacity to satisfy your needs as a learner. That is, 'evaluation' can provide you with one 'value', a definition of what the material is meant to convey, while at the same time permit you to derive another 'value' – the meaning that it has for you as a learner undertaking a particular course of study. In this way, the first meaning informs your learning, you come to know what the thing is, while the second meaning allows you to recognise its worth to you.

Of course, the first of these can be straightforward, but the second can prove a little troublesome: knowing some material is one thing, knowing whether it's ever going to prove of any real use to you is quite another; it's our perceptions of this potential use that often influence us most when it comes to learning anything. For instance, if you were presented with 10 topics to study and you were interested in six of them, but you knew the other four were going to be presented in an examination, which topics would you spend time on? The values we assign to learning material can serve not only to alter our perceptions but can also channel our behaviour in certain ways, which requires us to take care with any evaluation we pursue in weighing up the results of analysis. Evaluation might serve a dual purpose, but each has to be beneficial to you as a learner.

Embedded in the concepts of analysis and evaluation are the notional activities each of them require – investigation and reflection. With the intent to pursue a search for meaning in what is presented for us to learn, we must be equally committed to developing an awareness of how this learning might change us and how we will put it to use. Without in some way monitoring our responses to learning, and measuring the changes in our knowledge and behaviour, we lose the opportunity to get the most from any learning experience. It can be said that there is usually no shortage of yardsticks for testing a learner's understanding – all kinds of assessments are used on most courses, from examination papers to original research papers, and all of them may be informative for the learner in gauging their performance on a course. We might consider that where course assessments are staged events planned on a certain schedule, what feedback is available for the learner in the periods between? *Ad hoc* input from teachers and peers aside, the individual learner has to develop an awareness of personal performance in their learning, in essence to acquire the habit of investigating their own knowledge base and reflecting on how this informs their activity as a learner. A learner who never pauses to give any thought to the person at the centre of their learning – themselves – and who fails to question their own activities, runs the risk of having no control over their situation should things go wrong. More importantly, there is a very real danger of learning being replaced by rites and ritual behaviour, patterns of activity which, when overset, can produce a great many problems for the individual seeking to create a new stable base which was formed from passivity in the first place.

READING

Reading is a skill, one which you acquired a long time ago and are using at this moment while wondering why it should be highlighted here, especially after all that stuff about analysis and evaluation. What more do you need to know about reading than that you can read this?

The answer is – not a lot, but it should help increase your awareness of what you should consider when you read.

Attention

Pay close attention to what you read. Soak it up, let nothing get by you. And the best way to do that is to pay very close attention to your reading habits. What kind of reader are you? If your reading speed matches your ability to comprehend written information, you're all set. But can you honestly say that's the case? Consider the following.

- Does everything you're required to read interest you equally?
- Do you find some information more difficult to read than other kinds?
- Do you remember some written material more easily than other kinds?

It might be that since you learned to read, you've read so much and so often that you no longer pay attention to the way in which you read and ignore the host of factors which might have a bearing on how well you read. You might be aware that you seem to be a 'slow' or a 'fast' reader, but are you an *attentive* reader? If you were stopped halfway through a chapter of a book, and asked questions about what you've just read, how well would you do? You might do poorly or very well; it all depends on how you as a reader are 'managing' your attention and whether or not you are receptive to the information present in the material.

When it comes to participating in an educational course, though, you have to recognise that these attributes of attention and receptivity are vital: you're reading in order to learn, and that's the nub of the whole matter. *What* you read is important – *how* you read it is fundamental to your success in acquiring information that you need to have.

You have to pay attention then to what you read, make the effort to be ready to learn. If you find some of the material you must read as dry as dust and half as interesting, then you must be doubly sure that you remain receptive to it. That's easy to say, but it's so important you must keep it in mind; you have to stay open to information and ensure that none of it is blocked out by personal likes and dislikes, by mistaken notions that you're not 'smart' enough to handle it, or by intellectual inertia. If you convince yourself that written material is 'boring' or 'beyond you' it can be one of the hardest things in the world to open a book. Don't allow yourself to fall into traps like this. Paying attention to what you bring to reading and paying attention to what you read are two basic building blocks to learning. You can't afford to skimp on either.

Time

When you're absorbed in reading something, where does the time go? Hours pass like minutes. On the other hand, when you're grinding your frustrated way through material you dislike, an hour is forever. I can't tell you how to find everything you read absorbing, although a few suggestions are made below about the attempt to be interested. What I can point out is that no matter what you read, reading it will take time.

That hardly seems like a startling insight, but think about it for a while. If you have seven chapters of a giant book to get through, you're not going to do so without spending time at it. Make up your mind now that when it comes to reading you're going to behave like a sensible person and apportion realistic periods of time to acquiring information. Educational material can never be skimped; reading your way through a course starts at the beginning and never stops until you come out the other end, successfully.

The time you give to reading anything depends on two factors: (a) the ease with which you assimilate the information contained, and (b) the importance attached to it on the course.

So far as your ease of assimilation is concerned, you're the only person who can know this for sure, using feedback measures to test your understanding – from informal quizzing of yourself to formal assessment results. Whatever yardstick you use to test this assimilation, this learning, use it accurately and never fool yourself with the outcome. If it turns out that you have a flair for understanding whatever the subject read might be, fine. If not, don't ignore it. Apportion reading time accordingly, where the major factor for dealing with any problem in assimilation is to create *'re-reading'* time. Never, ever, be reluctant to read and re-read material. Your aim is to let information sink in, and however long it takes you, that's the time you should give it. You can parcel this time up into a number of 'tries', whatever suits you, but you must do it because it's time well spent; and don't waste a moment on chastising yourself for not grasping every nuance of the material at the first go – too many factors influence the accessibility of written information for you to single yourself out and shout 'Fool!'.

The importance of what you read, so far as learning aims and outcomes of the course you're taking go, should be reasonably obvious. If they're not, get this area straightened out. You must come clearly to grips with what you *need* to know and when you need to know it. We'll return to this later but for now, you have to form a very good idea of which material must not be avoided.

I use the word 'avoided' advisedly. It can be terribly easy for us to spend vast amounts of time reading our favourite subjects and let the virtuous glow of this 'studying' make righteous the claim that we have no time left over for reading anything else, especially when that 'anything else' signifies the subjects that give us nightmares. No one can force you to read and learn. Not even you. What you can do is set appropriate time aside to put yourself in front of the books and *try*. And keep trying. Whether it takes you five minutes or an hour to make sense of one passage or even one sentence, you have to spend this time anyway – so build it in to your studying, acknowledge it as being necessary, and then stop letting it distract you.

Interaction

If you could memorise information just by reading it through once, life would be much simpler. You can't; our minds don't work that way. But even if you had the ability of Marvo the Miracle Memory Person, what use would it be to you if all you could do was regurgitate undigested reams of material? Where's the learning? Information you acquire has to be handled in various ways before you can use it appropriately. Leaving aside the cognitive exercise your brain takes in processing this information, you can be certain of just one factor here – you are not about to learn a great deal from reading if you put your mind in neutral while you turn the pages.

If you're paying attention to what you're reading and giving yourself sufficient time to get acquainted with the material, you've already started doing this last vital activity of *interacting* with information that should be acquired. Let yourself think about what you're reading, ponder it, consider it carefully: is it completely new to you or does it fit somewhere with what you already know; how does it strike you, how do you react to it, does it put you adrift and prompt the realisation that you're lacking the basic data you need to understand it fully, or does it create a new insight for you; do you find the meaning crystal clear or fuzzy? All of this can be summed up in terms of how you are interacting with what you read. For the moment, don't concern yourself with trying to remember it – do your level best to *understand* it. Consciously handle the information, don't let each successive line, page or chapter slip by without being 'acted on' in some way. Put the book down and try to summarise what you've read, paraphrase a particularly 'difficult' passage – out loud. *Do* something with the information coming in.

When you deal with written information in an active way, it has a better chance of 'taking'. Opportunities are created for you to make it your own, to explore it and 'explain' it to yourself, to elicit whatever meaning you can derive from it and then discover what contribution to your learning that meaning has for you.

Certainly, all of this interacting can be easier to do if you're naturally interested in what you're reading. Being absorbed in reading material that you find suits you is a bonus; but what about the reams of information that you don't find conducive to your likes? You still have to read it and it's even more important that you make a conscious decision not to skimp on it in terms of the time and attention you give to it. However, even in accepting this, some subjects might seem virtually unassailable because we perceive them as possessing characteristics that act like 'off switches' to our minds. The result is that as soon as we decide that this subject or that is in some way a problem for us, dredging up the effort to learn about it can prove next to impossible.

So, here's how to do the impossible: first, get it straight in your head that neither you nor your 'pet hate' subject is at fault – no one and nothing is to be blamed – don't punish yourself and don't reject or avoid the material.

Second, behave towards the subject according to the importance it has for you as a learner, make the effort necessary to deal with it *no matter how you feel about it* – in other words, act as though you found it interesting and accessible; it's amazing how often appropriate attitudes (and feelings) can stem from 'doing' the appropriate behaviour. We might be more comfortable in believing it should be the other way round, that when the 'desire' to study particular material somehow magically washes over us *then* we'll start – but that's a snare and a delusion. Just get started anyway. Act.

Third, reward yourself in some way whenever you spend time on reading (and interacting) with material you find 'difficult'. Give yourself a bit of recognition for having accomplished a task you might have shirked, treat yourself well for having done so. The point about this 'reward system' is that it will act as a prompt for you to do what's necessary in the early stages of acquiring the habit of handling your problem subjects, and the fact that it's patently a 'trick' to get your head down and read is neither here nor there. You're setting up a workable situation in order to gain desirable consequences. It doesn't matter how it comes about so long as it happens.

I'd like to be able to end here by assuring you that if you stick it out, no subject will fail to interest you, but of course I can't. It might happen that way and it might not. The only certainty we have here is that no matter what demands any subject makes on you, the decision to engage your attention and make the necessary effort lies with you. If you have to continually deploy stratagems and ruses to do whatever's necessary, then it's just a matter of finding and using the ones which work. In the end, that's all that counts.

Before going on to discuss writing, I should link reading with that indispensable activity of any learner.

Using the library

I don't propose here to provide a route map for using the facilities of any good library, for the simple reason that any good librarian will do a much better job of it on the spot with the overwhelming benefit of both of you being in close proximity to the items and services that are provided. What I can do is to underscore some issues that are essential for you as a learner who will make good use of libraries. Let me repeat that – *you are a learner who will make good use of libraries.* Don't be offended, it needs to be said. For an awful lot of learners, libraries are quiet places where a person can daydream undisturbed, where the presence of textbooks and journals, indexes and abstracts, reports and reference volumes, and impressive hardware with disks recording more referenced material and data handling programs than you could shake a stick at, offers a pleasing background of compressed learning that serves to convince the onlooker that the learner is not idling.

So, if you haven't already had a guided tour of the library you will use most often, arrange one now. I have yet to meet an unhelpful librarian, and I am always astounded at the depth of knowledge they display in their field of expertise. If you thought people who worked in libraries were there just to make sure books were replaced on the right shelves, think again. You can never hope to handle library facilities as well as the person who knows them inside out. Put yourself in front of a good librarian and they'll put you in front of what you need to know. Never, ever, forget to appreciate them. At the very least, say 'Thank You' very nicely; they're going to save you a lot of time, and stop you wandering up and down the aisles between shelves, bamboozled.

Now that you've introduced yourself to the librarian, and they have kindly introduced you to the means by which you can tap the great reservoir of information their library contains, what's next? How will you go about using your time there?

The answer is – constructively. If you're heading for a library in need of nothing more than a quiet place to spread the books and study, fine. Get there, sit down and start. Ignore the interesting front pages on the journal stands and limit conversations to hello. Take out the books and immerse yourself.

If, on the other hand, you're going there to fill out some deficit in your knowledge base, be prepared. Define what you need: a particular textbook or journal? material contained on PC disks? Whatever your need might be, specify it as closely as possible, write it down if you like, and if you're at all unsure of where to lay your hands on the information you require – go first to the librarian and ask for help. If you have a clear idea of where to look and how to obtain your information go straight to it and get started.

This all sounds so simple and obvious. Why am I going on about it? Because for some of us, libraries aren't the warm and supportive havens that other learners find them. They're daunting places filled with acres of books and brainy people who stare at intruders and smirk at their obvious unease.

If you harbour any perception like this, dump it and dump it now. Tell that bit of yourself that finds libraries unsettling that you're going to go ahead and spend time in them anyway, you're going to get used to approaching librarians and asking for help and you're going to get used to the knowledge that you've every right to be there. The library was created for you to use, that's the bottom line – it exists to serve your needs.

WRITING FOR A READER

Early on in your course you have to come to grips with the fact that you will be required to produce written material that will be read (and assessed) by someone else. Leaving aside the vexing question of the quality of the content for now, we can assume that whatever you write it has to be *readable*. This 'readability' can be broken down into two approaches – Legibility and Logic.

Legibility

We'll take examinations first, where you might be required to produce 'essay' type answers of several hundred words in length. You might be able to hand in other written assessment material produced on a type-writer or PC at other times in your course (see below) but for formal exams, it's just you, your pen and blank sheets of paper.

So, exactly how bad is your handwriting? Are you often complimented on the artistic clarity of your penmanship? If you are, how long does it usually take you to produce an admirable script? Too long for an exam setting? And if your usual standard of handwriting is an illegible scrawl that needs deciphering, what happens to it when you're under pressure? How skilled does any reader need to be in cryptography before they can make any sense of it?

If you're in the first category, take an average question paper set on your course that requires essay answers, choose a question you are confident of making a full and detailed answer in and have a go at it. Time how long it takes you to do so – if you're within the allotted time span for the question and your script is still clear and beautiful, good. If not, and while you're satisfied with the extent of the answer but it took you far too long to produce a clear hand, think carefully about your willingness to sacrifice marks for extra material in exchange for congratulations about your handwriting style. If you found pressure of time destroys your legibility, join the other scribblers and read on.

Rules for Scribblers

1. Never forget you're writing for a reader whom you must never, ever, offend with the poor quality of your handwriting. That reader has precious marks to dispense and the undeniable prerequisite for the accumulation of sufficient marks to pass an examination is that examiners must be able to read your answers.

2. If your handwriting is poor because you're too lazy to bother improving it, think carefully about the entire matter again. If your handwriting is abysmal because you really never learned to make it regular or because you just fell into the scribbling habit, correct it.

    Writing, like reading, is one of those skills we sometimes think is not so much a skill as it is a personality trait. We write poorly or we write well, that's it; but of course it's not; writing is easily practised, we just have to make ourselves accept the idea that it's worthwhile to practise writing clearly. Why should other people be expected to spend time trying to make sense of the illegible scrawl you produce – the packed collection of straight lines interrupted by the occasional dot or squiggle, or the dense little arches looped together with no spaces in between? Especially when those 'other people' are examiners with 50 or more scripts to mark?

3. If you're uncertain about how clear your handwriting is, try this: ask a friend to read over some of your notes – that's right, notes, not some painfully put-together sample of your best handwriting efforts. Have them try to read notes you made during a lecture or when studying, because these will probably be fairly representative of how you write under pressure of time. Have these notes read by someone who isn't familiar with the subject of the notes. Then ask them to read the material *aloud*.

Now, this is a tough test of your legibility, but if they can't read from the material at a reasonable speed, if there is a high incidence of false starts and stumbles and remarks like 'What's this here – is this a word or a doodle?' then it's time to practise making your handwriting clearer. Being able to communicate first requires a mastery of the form the communication will take. Here, with writing for an examiner squarely in mind, we don't have to be ashamed to note some very basic tips for encouraging legibility:

(a) Get yourself a pen you feel comfortable with, one that produces a smooth and unbroken flow of ink that doesn't blot. Don't be tempted to reject advice as simple as this. If your handwriting is bad news, you need all the help you can get.

(b) Learn to write in straight lines, for the simple reason that a lot of essay answers are expected to be provided on unlined paper. If you 'naturally' write on the slant, correct this. If you find you absolutely can't master horizontal writing on blank paper, try this – take a lined piece of paper and insert it under the blank sheet so that when you press down to write you can stick to the lines showing through. Don't, even for a second, be reluctant to do this in an exam: rule off a set of lines on scrap paper and use them. Your finished script will benefit and that's all that counts.

(c) Stick to printed margins provided on exam answer paper. Don't meander through them or use them for script headings. They're put there for the examiner's use, not yours. Take care to set down each successive line of script next to the margin; a lot of people acquire the habit of writing succeeding lines of script just a little further to the right than the one before. It looks odd. Stick to the margin.

(d) Correct mistakes neatly. To err is human, to scrape holes in an exam paper when covering up mistakes is outrageous. Nobody expects you to produce a perfect response with every word perfectly placed first time. We can all make mistakes; examiners expect to see them. If your corrections are neat and unobtrusive, there's no harm done. Just draw a line through the word, words or paragraphs you want to correct from the first letter to the last and move on.

By the same token of clarity, if, on rereading an exam answer you wish to insert a word, or even a whole line, into the script, do so with care and remember to indicate to the examiner where this extra wordage is to be read in conjunction with the rest of the script – use a plain symbol such as an asterisk or little arrow.

One last point about handwriting and exams: it takes nothing less than brilliance and originality to astound examiners so much that they will be willing to plough through a tediously scrawled answer in order to decipher the nuggets of genius that are hidden among the debris. If you can guarantee to produce just such works of genius every time, then maybe you can afford to scribble your illegible way through exams. If not, learn to write clearly. Your handwriting doesn't have to be perfect, but it should be readable.

Now apart from exams, you may be required to produce written material for course assessments – essays, projects, reports and so on. If you have to write these by hand, then the suggestions made above all apply, and you might be allowed even less leeway in the legibility stakes since you will have had sufficient time to prepare the material. However, in these cases, you have the opportunity to consider submitting finished work in printed form, and I would strongly recommend, even if your course doesn't make it mandatory, that you do so. Whether typed or produced on a PC, legibility of this finished work can hardly be bettered. If you don't have access to a PC with a word-processing package or a typewriter, then think seriously about how you might gain that access.

Word-processing PCs might be outside your budget, but good typewriters might not be and second-hand reconditioned machines can be bought fairly cheaply. If you're really stuck, do you know anyone who would be willing to type up a manuscript for you or print it from a PC? Be charming and beg if you have to, and don't forget to offer to pay for the paper. Of course, if you're required to prepare and submit a series of 5000-word essays, you can go to the well too often and friendly support from a typing friend can dry up just when you need it most. It might be easier and safer to scrimp for a typewriter of your own and learn to peck away at it until you produce tidy scripts.

Logic

Don't be too concerned about my use of the word 'logic' here. These passages are about straightforward issues in producing sensible written material, that's all. Nothing fancy.

First, a word to the frightened: you're not alone. Large numbers of people experience great reluctance in setting their knowledge down on paper. Sometimes the 'reason' is simple – they can't spell, or stringing sentences together gives them the heebie-jeebies. In other cases, the 'reason' is much more complex; over time, they have convinced themselves that they are incapable of writing anything worthwhile, their self-esteem is very low and it has become much easier just to avoid writing anything longer and more demanding than a note to the milkman. More insidiously, and unforgivably, some people are convinced by others – usually incompetent teachers at school – that they will never be able to write; they have no capacity for it and have nothing worthwhile to say, certainly nothing that anyone would be interested in.

If you place yourself in the first category, you know that with an effort you can acquire the skills necessary to improve your confidence. If you place yourself in the second category then please believe me, it's all nonsense. Every single one of us can learn to write well; it just takes time and practice to learn how to set your thoughts down on paper in a fashion that other people can make sense of. You are not the exception to this statement. With effort and commitment you can do it. In fact, the odds are that you're already capable of it, but the long-lasting effects of a seriously bad school experience prevents you from realising it.

I'm droning on about this for good reason. Making sense on paper will be a required activity on your course and will consume enough intellectual energy without any of it being side-tracked into worrying over the nonsense some fool fed you years ago. So, if you're carrying any psychological baggage around with you about what you think you *can't* do with your writing, set it down and walk away from it without a backward glance.

Let's start with a few misapprehensions about the writing you'll do for assessments: It doesn't have to be (a) brilliantly original, or (b) perfect – these are *not* the standards that will be expected of you. Your teachers and examiners just want some proof submitted to them that suggests your brain is in use and you're benefiting from the course as a learner. That's it. The written material you provide for assessment purposes is not going to be scrutinised by an array of cynics who are desperate to laugh at your grammar. Trust them to treat you fairly, because they invariably will.

Now, what experience do you have in writing essays and reports, compiling material for special projects? Very little? Then go out of your way to acquire it. Get writing and practise; writing is one of those skills that *always* benefits from rehearsal; it never goes stale, it always improves. While you're practising, keep the following recommendations in mind.

Grammar, Syntax, Clauses and Things

If English is your first language, you've probably acquired many habits in using it that you know you really should try to correct. If you've learned English as a second language, your grammar is probably better than mine. In either case, if you feel the need, go out and buy a DIY guide to using English and take pains over producing 'correct' English. By all means, feel free.

So far as we're concerned here, however, we'll be discussing the approximate shapes of written material, not grammatical nuts and bolts. If you can pin sentences together that say what you want them to say, and other people take out of them the meaning you intended, what more do you need? Probably just a mixture of confidence and practice.

Words

Buy two good dictionaries: one for 'ordinary' English, one for the 'technical' terminology you will use. Make constant use of both of them to define clearly all of those words that you *think* you know the meaning of. When you come across a word new to you, look it up and take notes.

If you can't spell well, learn to do so. Check your writing against the dictionary. The onus is on you to convey information accurately, and that includes spelling words the way everybody else does.

Using big words where small ones would do is a terrible temptation. Avoid it. If small words express your meaning clearly, stick with them.

Don't become a Jargonaut. In any profession, technical terms are created for use between members in a kind of descriptive shorthand, a professional 'jargon'. The correct use, in an appropriate context, of this jargon is acceptable. Larding your conversation and writing with it in order to impress people is not. Use specialised words only where no other words would convey your meaning, especially when you're not *totally* familiar with every nuance that the jargon might suggest. Remember that your writing will be read by individuals who are likely to be much more aware of what the jargon means than you are – if your use of it is misapplied, out of context or just plain pretentious, you'll be striking the wrong note. Never attempt to conceal ignorance with jargon; an expert can floor you with the simple query – 'What does that word mean, exactly?'

Sentences

Use short sentences wherever possible. Seriously long sentences make prisoners of both writer and reader. Use them only when you must. Avoid them when you can.

Paragraphs do more than tidy up a page. When bits of information need to be separated for clarity's sake, start a new paragraph. Paragraphs become too long when they ramble from one point to another in sentences that have no obvious connections between them.

Never be afraid to write a very short paragraph.

Sequences

Always have a 'sequence' in mind when writing anything, from a single sentence to a paragraph to a 20-page essay. Lead from one point to another and make sure every word contributes to the sense of the whole.

Sometimes, the topic you're writing about will suggest a 'natural' sequence of its own; for example, the history of Nursing Registration, where the natural sequence may be drawn from a timetable of events. More often, and annoyingly, no 'natural' sequence is immediately apparent. In this case, 'sequence' becomes part and parcel of the way you choose to identify and develop the 'theme' of your writing, and this 'thematic' approach is dealt with in detail in Chapter 4.

For the moment, we can note that imposing a sequence on writing is the way in which you 'tell the story' that you want to impart, so that your message is taken to point C via points A and B, saying all the things you want to say and giving the reader a chance to follow your train of thought without getting lost.

Rewriting

Preparing drafts of written material is covered elsewhere in this book, but it can be emphasised here that the habit of rewriting anything you've written is an extremely valuable one to acquire. Try the following.

1. Choose a topic about which you're particularly knowledgeable and write 500 words about it. Put in specific points of information, facts and figures.
2. Now try to compress what you've written to just 250 words, *without* omitting any of the points you raised in the original piece, and while still ensuring that it makes sense.

The major point here is that the first attempt we make at writing anything that is intended to convey a reasonable amount of information often contains a major flaw – we know *what* we want to say but we're not sure about *how* to say it. A common result of this is that we say too much. Rewriting material gives us the opportunity to *rethink* and *restate* our messages.

So far your thoughts about writing have been turned outwards, towards a reader. Now we can focus attention on you, the writer writing for yourself, and address that activity dear to the heart of any student – note-taking.

Take note and take care

The purpose of note-taking is to summarise text, speech or thought. To compress down all the oceans of data that will confront you on your course into a form that you can manage and into amounts that you can use. In those last two points are contained the rationale for ensuring that you make and take notes wisely and well; which might be restated as – what *type* of notes will you make and to what *purpose* will you put them?

Selectivity

Being selective about the notes you make depends a good deal on the source of material you use. The most significant factor about these sources is the kind of *access* you have to the information they deliver. We can split this notion of access into two dimensions – temporary and permanent.

People are *temporary* sources of information. In lectures and discussions, items of information can be presented to you just once, briefly and at speed. You have to be awake and aware, ready to make notes which are concise, precise and accurate. This can be difficult to achieve, but it's not impossible to do. Unless you know shorthand, taking down remarks verbatim can take your attention completely off what's being said. It's much better in this situation to make selective 'headings' of material presented that you will use as a series of signposts or guidelines for pursuing further study. Good teachers will emphasise particular points of interest and these can form the backbone of your notes. Essentially, you're attempting to establish nothing more than an *outline* of what you've heard, one that will trigger off more detailed learning later.

Text is a *permanent* source of information. You can refer back to books and journals and so on to verify the accuracy of information you've obtained from them. In this case, you have much more time at your disposal and your notes can reflect this. Besides providing you with a 'digest' of written information, note-taking from text can be an invaluable learning tool if you paraphrase what you read. Putting textual material into your own words as you compose your notes requires you to consider the information carefully, to interact with it.

Whatever the situation that prompted them, what do you do with your notes once they're made? The first thing to do is transcribe them into as clear a form as you can.

Transcription: quality versus quantity

Taking temporary source notes first, write them out again *as soon as you can* after the lecture or discussion is over. Don't put it off for long because you might forget what was talked about, and you want to clothe the bare skeleton of your notes with as much detail as you can recall. Write them out in full in the order in which they were made, and use each 'heading' as a prompt to preface your written recollections of what was said. With practice you'll be surprised at how much you can remember, *if* you do this 'rounding-out' exercise quickly enough after the event.

When you're satisfied that you've got a reasonable record of information you've heard, go to an authoritative source to check the detail and accuracy of the substance of your notes. Then start filling in the learning picture by acquiring more information.

Permanent source notes are a different matter, and we can suggest that all notes we make from these sources, since they might prove to be the only 'permanent' record we use for the material thereafter, have to be complete, and they have to be accurate. Here then, where temporary source notes are primarily concerned with quality of information, we have to be concerned from the beginning with both quality and quantity.

It is all too easy, when taking notes from text, to bunch your notes up at one extreme or the other and record too much or nowhere near enough. At the beginning of your studies there is no easy way for you to tell these two states apart; only time and experience can really guide you. However, bear one point in mind as a rule of thumb – if you were to return to a set of notes after a prolonged period, do they contain enough information for your needs? Without the rehearsal of information that reading and re-reading a text while making notes provides, key points that we thought we knew can fade beyond recall. Notes from text have to be complete and thoroughly reflect the original information from which they are taken.

One last point: as time goes by you will accumulate an ever-increasing amount of personal notes. Take care to keep them organised, treat them as a valuable source of information. Read them, revise and update them.

The last skills we'll talk about here deal briefly with your experience of being a learner and how you might approach these.

NAVIGATING A COURSE

Read all about it. Get hold of a detailed copy of your course curriculum and become very familiar with the contents. Learn what will be expected of you and when: how is the course organised – where, when and how are topics presented; what methods of assessment will be used and where do these assessments occur in the course schedule? No part of the course should take you by surprise, get ready for it.

If you experience any problems with your learning, shout for help. Don't stay silent and fail. Most institutions provide learners with a nominated study support/counselling service. Make good use of it. If no formal arrangements of this kind are made locally, approach a member of the teaching staff and establish just how you can have access to help if you need it. The best time to make this approach is *before* you find you're up to your neck in trouble.

Whenever you need help, then, don't hesitate to ask for it. When it's offered, take it. Remember that this help, if it is to be of any use to you, will still require your participation, your efforts to make it work. Act on the help you're given.

If you've come up against some problems with your course, met them head on and worked towards a resolution for them, don't waste a moment in looking back. Go forward. No part of any course can suit everyone. Don't blame yourself, don't despair, don't drag your feet by worrying about it. Get stuck in.

3 Using textbooks and journals

The majority of information you will acquire on your course will come from a collection of specialist textbooks and journals. You won't have to fritter away your time searching through libraries deciding on which of these to use (at least not in the early stages of your education) because course leaders will provide you with a 'Recommended Reading' list, which will probably be supplemented from time to time with individual teachers' own suggestions.

These reading lists will contain the names of all the main textbooks you need on your course, selected on the basis that they supply the 'prime messages' the course is intended to convey. This term, 'prime message', should be explained a little.

Your participation in your course must be carefully guided; you must be given a solid footing in the knowledge you require, be guided through material in successive stages at the right time and in the right way, so that you may arrive at a state of learning in which the foundations of your knowledge base allow you to both handle and use the information you have and equip you to carry on learning in the appropriate acquisition and use of more knowledge. This means that you should be encouraged to grasp information correctly, wholly and completely aware of what it has to teach you in a logical and progressive way. The texts recommended to you (bolstered by lectures and other presentations) will contain information that embody the 'prime messages' which course organisers believe you should know, where these messages are at once a source of knowledge and the signposts you should follow in order to align your learning with what you need it to do for you.

'Recommended Reading' lists should be treated with due care and attention. In all likelihood, teachers will spend time going through these lists with you, pointing out the advantages of using them properly. Listen carefully to what they have to say. Take notes. Buy the books you're told are indispensable; they may be expensive (they probably will be expensive) but do your level best. Library stocks are always an option, of course, but you don't want to find that a trip to your library to borrow an 'indispensable' book is fruitless because everybody else got there before you. Besides, extended loans on some books are impossible to obtain – if you take out a popular book you might not be allowed to retain it for more than a few weeks.

Building up a personal stock of textbooks can be done piecemeal so long as you follow a sensible order in doing so. After acquiring the indispensable texts, take advice from teachers as to which to buy next. The obvious choices you will have to make will depend on just where in the syllabus a subject is introduced that requires you to have the recommended text. Sometimes, though, things aren't so clear-cut; perhaps a teacher suggests that you acquire a book 'early' so take advice where you can. Don't forget that most cities have educational bookstores dotted around them that might be able to provide you with second-hand copies of books you need at greatly reduced prices. A word of caution, though, about buying second-hand; be *very* careful to buy the correct *edition* of the textbook you need; 'reprints' are okay; a new *edition* means that the text has been revised and updated. You don't want to be working from the wrong book; the title might be the same, but it will still be the wrong book.

Journals are a different matter. Where course organisers recommend that you read a specific journal (or journals) you can always rely on finding these in good libraries, at least for as long as it takes you to photocopy the material you will need; but remember that if a single journal is recommended, a year's personal subscription can be had for about the same price as a comprehensive textbook. It's worth investing in a good journal: the information is absolutely up-to-date and reasonably brief. Naturally, at the beginning of your course the contents might be a bit beyond you, so concentrate on your books first and journal material afterwards.

With a set of recommended textbooks to hand, and access to journals arranged, you're ready to start soaking up the knowledge. Here, you can pause for a while to consider some points:

- not all information is accurate;
- not all information is 'true'.

Now, a cynic might suggest that if your course teachers present any information to you as being either accurate or 'true' then it would be an extremely unwise learner who didn't behave as though they believed what they were being told. We can handle that cynical point of view by suggesting that any information presented to you in good faith as being either accurate, or 'true', or both, can be dealt with by you in the same frame of mind, whether that information comes to you via teachers or texts. As time goes by and your store of knowledge gains in substance and depth, you will come to apply your own checks and balances to the weighing-up of the accuracy and veracity of information, and you will learn that some data is amenable to scientific testing to establish accuracy and some data might as well be served up on a plate and tasted for personal preference, to be swallowed whole, chewed over or left untouched. As for truth, it's too closely tied up with *allegiance* and *belief* for you to treat it with anything other than caution.

In a nutshell – any information which you accept and use, and which you don't personally 'prove' or otherwise verify, is accepted on faith.

This 'faith' in knowledge is what virtually all of us get by on. There isn't world enough and time for us to go 'proving' everything we learn, but there is a great difference between acting on faith and being trapped in the cages of dogmatism. You might never 'prove' any single piece of information, but you can still evaluate it: you can and should desire to learn to tell fact from fiction, theory from assumption, workable concepts from half-baked suppositions. Your knowledge base is one thing, your powers of discrimination are another. Build them up over time and remember that you never lose the right to question.

TEXTBOOKS

The function of textbooks is to be *instructive*, to supply information in particular ways so that it may be assimilated and learned from. This information should be presented, described and explained so as to deliver clear and unequivocal messages, which are germane to the subject and never stray from their purpose. In other words, textbooks are meant to teach. If all teaching is the means by which learning is expedited, textbooks should do just that.

Some do. Some don't.

The best textbooks are clearly and simply written, moving in well-ordered sequences in which the only complexity that may be found arises from the nature of the material. The worst textbooks make complete sense only to their authors. Why am I banging on like this? Because I want you to know, if you don't already, that no subject is impossible for you to grasp. There is you, and there is the information you need to learn, and the only problems that can arise in bridging the gap between you and it will stem from the medium through which the information is presented and the commitment you bring to your learning. If you know that no effort is beyond you, then you must pay attention to the sources of your learning, and come to understand how your acquisition of information may be influenced by the means through which you approach it.

So, if you find the messages in the textbook opaque, and you just can't get into the material, *never* jump to the conclusion that it's because you're stupid. It might be that you don't have the grounding in the subject that you should have – in which case you can start with a simpler text and remedy any deficiency. It might be that some internal state of your own is preventing you learning, a fear of failure perhaps, for which the only solution is to get your head straight and renew your efforts. Or it might be that the textbook is a badly written jumble of obstacles to understanding.

If you can recognise that learning is encouraged or hindered by influences other than some imagined lack of intelligence on your part, and take steps to produce and strengthen the positive, encouraging influences, nothing is beyond you. That includes mastering the contents of your textbooks.

In a straightforward perspective, we'll look at how textbooks are generally arranged and how you can make good use of them.

CONTENTS, INDEX, BIBLIOGRAPHY

Contents

The contents of textbooks are *organised* in certain ways, based on the author's perceptions of how the material is related one item to another and how the whole should be presented. That sounds simple enough, but a cautious learner should take nothing for granted. Familiarise yourself with *how* material is actually presented. Does the author move from straightforward 'basic' issues and go on to build up towards more detailed information? Or are involved and intricate ideas presented first, so that they may be taken apart and inspected? Is one method used throughout the book, or a mixture of both? Never make the assumption that because the *subject* of the book would seem to lend itself to one particular type of presentation, this is how it will be written about in the book. You might end up floundering around in what seems to you to be a mass of disconnected material. There will be some order to it, you just have to look for it and then follow it as best you can.

The organisation of content is one thing, the substance of it is another.

Style

Some authors write very lucidly and make even the densest material accessible. Some could barely give you instructions on how to get to the end of your street. The difference between these two types of authors has very little to do with how much they know and everything to do with how they express that knowledge. Some write well, constructing messages for learners. Others slap the material down and expect you to dig through it. You just have to come to terms with this last group of authors. The demands that each make of you as a reader are, in the long run, only important if you come to dismiss the first as too simple and the second as too difficult. Aim to welcome the lucid writer's style and be patient with the one who can't write. Both have something to say.

Coherence

Writing coherently goes a little beyond style in that a coherent text allows you to follow the author's train of thought through the presentation of the material. You might have to take things at a slow pace, but you know where you've been, where you're going, and you'll know where you are when you get there. This can be a very troublesome effect for authors to create, so don't expect it from everyone.

Coherence in a text confers a certain shape upon it that you will recognise and can follow. If you find any textbook that seems incoherent to you, it might be the case that you will have to 'reshape' the information you acquire, where this 'reshaping' is the product of your growing knowledge about the subject. Again, have patience. Just because you find your interaction with a text to be problematic, it doesn't automatically mean the fault lies with you.

Jargon and the fog index

Aside from the appropriate and 'unavoidable' use of technical terminology, some authors seem to revel in cramming every page of a textbook with opaque jargon and jaw-cracking polysyllabic monster words. The usual result is to render any message either elusive in the extreme or ambiguous to the point of being misleading. There's not a great deal you can do about this, except to read such a text in parallel with two good dictionaries – one 'technical' and one 'general' – and hope that the meaning stays intact as you 'translate' the messages.

The point is that the nature of individual words as important components in a text has a vital contribution to make in ensuring that the overall meaning is accessible to the reader. Using any text to which you regularly find it difficult to gain access and understand can be a tedious and tiring business, and might result in your belief that the material is beyond your grasp. Well, if you just read it and reread it without 'translation' it could prove to be just that. However, you can bear in mind that some texts *are* 'badly' written, and this perception should help you to realise that the matter of gaining access to the material is an 'external' obstacle to your understanding, one that you can overcome with time and patience and practice. For interest's sake, we can look briefly at a system called the *Fog Index* which the American business teacher Robert Gunning derived as an approximate measure of how difficult a text might be to read and understand. This is how it works:

1. Choose an average page from a text and, starting and finishing at the beginning of one sentence and the end of another, take any passage of 100 words as your 'test' sample. Get as near to this figure as you can manage; note the total precisely. Now count the number of sentences in your sample: be careful about the author's use of punctuation – if any very long sentences occur with colons or semi-colons dividing them up, count these divisions as separate sentences *if* they stand up grammatically on their own.
2. Divide the exact number of words in the sample by the number of sentences. This gives the *average sentence length*.
3. Now count the number of long words in the sample which have three syllables or more. Don't include words which are extended to this length by the addition of '-es' or '-ed', or those which are made up of easy little words, such as 'specialist'.
4. Finally, add the number of long words to the average sentence length number. Multiply the result by 0.4 to arrive at the Fog Index for the sample text.

This Fog Index is an approximate measure of the minimum number of years of formal schooling which would be needed before a reader could understand the text. In the UK, a Fog Index of 13 would roughly reflect a Sixth Year stage in secondary education, and one of 16 a tertiary stage or degree level education. Now, remember that this *is* a rough guide, but you can see that any text which regularly attracts a Fog Index of 16 or more would make special demands on the reader. Where the figure of 18 is achieved and sustained for more than isolated sections of a book, the whole presentation of material could prove inaccessible to the majority of readers, regardless of how knowledgeable and well-educated they were.

I once applied this exercise to a book on conceptual models of nursing care and got a Fog Index of 22, which I must say reassured me more than a little, since it let me view my complete bewilderment in a new light. I finally came to grips with the text by 'translating' it in a series of small steps and by making a great many detailed notes, and I ended up learning from it. (The average Fog Index for *this* book is low, which I hope means my intention to make it an easy and fairly effortless read is successful.)

Using the Fog Index can be illuminating, but don't take it too seriously. A high Fog Index in a text should just prompt you to make an extra effort.

Exposition

As a learner, you might expect authors to make reasoned and reasonable expositions of the material they present. Many do, and take pains to place information in proper contexts, rounding out and substantiating the messages they provide. Some don't, and leave facts, figures, concepts and assertive statements hanging in mid-air with little introduction and no explanation. This happens, and it can be a potent recipe for half-grasped knowledge and outright misunderstanding.

You can recognise these latter texts when reading them keeps prompting you to say anything such as: 'Wait a minute, where did *that* come from?', 'What does this bit *mean*?', 'How does all this fit together?' and 'I'm missing something here': which you undoubtedly are, and it's not your fault. Lack of appropriate exposition makes for text where, no matter how often you read any passage and understand the words, the *meaning* still escapes you, because the meaning should have been embedded in the connections made between pieces of information. But wasn't. If you do discover a text or texts like this where, no matter how much effort you make, messages remain obscure and information seems to hang in mid-air without any visible means of support, then a different approach can be taken and you must read around the subject, obtain other books dealing with the same material and start developing another picture of what it means. This 'reading around' any subject is usually done after you've grasped the basics, but in some cases you have little choice, you've got to go to other sources before you can come to terms with the information.

If you do have to 'read around' anything, get the simplest and most straightforward texts you can. You want to create a quick access to the material. Don't hesitate to go for 'Primers' – very basic books – even if they *do* have large print and lots of diagrams. You can read them quickly and move on.

References, Bibliography, Index

Information which an author uses in a text may be drawn from a number of sources, and depending on the nature of this information, such as its degree of originality or 'authority', the writer will ascribe its 'ownership' to another author whose work is being used or 'referred' to in some way. This system of making reference to previous work on a subject is a feature of academic texts, and is intended both to present a sufficiently informed text and to include, identify and underscore what other writers in the field have to contribute to the material.

These references can be used in various ways. The two most commonly used systems are dealt with in detail in the next chapter of this book, but whichever system an author uses, it will be used throughout the whole text. The only difference you will find is that some texts have Reference Lists provided at the end of every chapter while others supply an extensive Reference List at the end of the book, usually sited just before the Bibliography.

A Bibliography is a collection of texts named by the author as having been a useful source of knowledge in preparing his or her own text, where the material has helped the author's understanding of the subject, but from which no item of information has been specifically taken for inclusion in the author's own work. Selected books in a Bibliography will sometimes be specially emphasised by the author on a 'Recommended Further Reading List'.

Indexes are the alphabetical list of items placed at the back of textbooks, naming particular items covered in the text and where to find them. These indexes are handy for finding your way to a specific topic and come in very useful when you're required to search for it through a number of texts.

JOURNALS

For too many of us, professional journals are those things we always mean to read regularly and thoroughly but seldom do. Yet no comparable source of relevant information is available: journals provide a medium for the transmission and sharing of knowledge that is current, pertinent and which might not otherwise come to your attention. They are vehicles for learning, and repay their proper use at even the earliest stages of your professional education.

Structure and Function

Journals come in all kinds of formats with a wide variety of contents, from the 'magazine' type with informative articles, reports, news stories and job advertisements, through 'specialist' publications for sections of the profession, to the ones which deal solely with research-based papers. Each and all of these have something to offer, whether produced in the domestic or foreign markets. There are literally hundreds to choose from, and any good college or university library will keep a regular stock of scores of examples.

Almost all professional journals rely on submisions from 'external' contributors to present material that reflects current thinking and practice in the profession, so that an up-to-date profile of professional knowledge may be offered to readers. Each of them will have an editorial purpose in how articles are selected for inclusion – so, as we've noted, some journals will concentrate exclusively on research activity, some will focus on a specific field of knowledge, others will present a fairly eclectic view on matters of common interest. Spend some time getting acquainted with a broad range of journals taken from each of these 'types' and develop an awareness of which publication offers which kind of material.

A word of advice: while the 'cutting edge' of professional knowledge is more often to be discovered in the scholarly papers found in research-based journals, don't dismiss the others for some perceived lack of learning value. A vast amount of readily accessible material is crammed into the less 'academic' publications, which can offer effortless stepping stones to worthwhile information gains. You might sometimes find a vein of professional snobbery expressed about some journals. Ignore it and make up your own mind about what will help you learn. The few notes below about the main contents of journals should help you do that.

Editorial comment and 'staff' writing apart, the texts you'll find in journals can be identified as falling into one of the categories below, each of which display certain characteristics. This is an approximate guide, and you can always find some material which crosses the 'boundaries' noted here, but generally speaking, most professional writing can be grouped under one of the following headings.

Feature articles

This type of article usually deals with a topic currently of general interest to large sections of the profession. A good example will provide a rounded digest of the subject presented, explain how it may affect the profession in some way, and inform the reader without striving to provide a detailed or in-depth knowledge of the topic. Some feature articles present balanced views, weigh up the pros and cons of some important issue; others might express a heavy bias and present a stream of the writers' opinions with little or no attempt at justification. Both of these approaches are perfectly legitimate in this type of writing, since no author in either of these perspectives (or any mixture of the two), is doing anything other than discussing the issue. Feature articles are the place for people to 'air their thoughts' and offer material for consideration and debate.

A variation on this kind of article is what might more properly be termed a 'commentary', where a discursive, explanatory 'essay-type' piece of writing deals with a single issue, usually a published text, which is of concern to the profession. The writer most often has an acknowledged expertise in the subject and is considered to be capable of making a pertinent examination of it for the benefit of others. The publication of Government Policy affecting the profession, for example, would prompt the publication of commentaries.

Critiques

A critique is exactly what it sounds like, a critical essay. Critiques come in many shapes and guises, and while the prime function is to provide a careful analysis and evaluation of the work of other people, the medium itself is sometimes conducive to the production of essays which are less balanced than they might be. Reading critiques can be a very useful way of obtaining a ready-made insight into some area of knowledge, which you can chew over at leisure. On the other hand, the strongest insight you gain might be into the degree of bias held by the writer of the critique, which in itself might be of some value. Critiques should deliver a cool appraisal of something so that you are helped towards an understanding of it, but it does no harm for you to read critiques with a 'secondary' intention of making your own appraisal of the contents.

Literature reviews

These are dealt with in detail in another chapter. For now we can note that these reviews aim to present accurate, comprehensive 'digests' of the material published on some particular suject. Good reviews can be of immense help to the learner in providing a wealth of information in a succinct format – one that also signposts the way towards acquiring access to a wider field of information.

Research papers

This is a 'catch-all' title, covering a number of different types of publication. Essentially, a research paper is a report of some research activity undertaken by the author(s). The form that this report takes should reflect the nature of the research that was done, and is governed by strict 'rules' which are intended to ensure a close observation of the need for objectivity and accuracy.

Any good report of research activity contains three essential components:

- a description of the research methods used and why these were chosen in this particular instance;

- a straightforward presentation of the research data;

- a note of any event or circumstance which 'limits' the research results in any way – for example, it is not unusual for authors to offer a word of caution with regard to how their work should be interpreted because they failed to properly address some facet of their research which they *now* know to be important and which might have influenced the outcome.

Certainly, published research papers include more information than this, but these are key issues and fundamentally affect how objectively and accurately the material is presented. The author is *obliged* to tell you these things so that you have important data in your possession which will help you to analyse and evaluate the report.

Research methodologies are many and various, selected for use on the basis of how appropriate they are to the work at hand, where this work is based on some form of *investigation*. Now, whether this investigation is a small-scale, non-experimental survey or a double-blind crossover clinical trial of huge dimensions, the mechanics of it must be demonstrated clearly so that the eventual results of the study may be placed in their proper context. In doing so, authors of research papers must strive to present their information in a traditionally acceptable way and write in an 'approved academic' style. It's this 'academic' style that can give rise to problems for the reader who is not familiar with it.

The first thing to realise about 'academic' research papers is that they adhere to a pattern, where successive stages are used as showcases for components of the reports. A common pattern might look like the following.

Abstract	A summary of the report
Introduction	Brief synopsis of the subject addressed; can include comments on the relevant field, justification for the research, method(s) used in the study
Description of research activity	Application of research methods
Presentation of data	Information gained from the study
Analysis of data	'Results' of research: may include forms of statistical analysis
Conclusions	Researcher's comments on the study findings
Recommendations	Researcher's comments on how the study findings might be used, possibly remarking on the need for further study in the field
Limitations	Identification of possible influences on the study and its outcomes

From beginning to end, the intention is to deliver a cool, detached stream of information which is as free from bias as the author(s) can manage. It is this attempt to remove all trace of undue or prejudiced influence from research activity reports which gives them both their very great and indispensable value to any body of knowledge and their apparent impenetrability to the novice reader. The last instance doesn't apply to every research paper, of course. Usually, it happens where papers are written with an extreme and highly cautious regard for 'truth' and where the numerical tools of statistical analysis are employed.

We'll take these two 'obstacles' to grasping the messages of research papers and explore them in a little detail.

Caution and 'truth'

As fundamental issues in the preparation of 'academic' reports, caution and 'truth' (which are discussed elsewhere in this book from your own perspective as an academic writer) must be handled with the intention to never knowingly compromise either the accuracy of the information, or any inherent 'value' it may have, by the manner of its presentation. In paying careful heed to this concept, academic writing departs from the more usual habits that people employ in communicating with each other, and tries to ensure that information is transmitted which is shorn of every possible unwarranted influence that might serve to confer a property upon it which it does not possess.

Taking 'normal' exchanges, for example: in conversation, you might tell me you're thinking of buying your first car, you're willing to spend £2000 on it, and do I have any thoughts on the matter? I say yes, and then proceed to tell you that:

(a) Absolutely the best second-hand car to buy is a Vauxhall Astra, white for preference, with less than 50,000 miles on the clock.
(b) The best examples of second-hand Astras are less than three years old, thereby costing nearer £4000 than £2000.
(c) The best place in town to buy second-hand cars is at the MotorMart on the Edinburgh Road, where the owner is honest and the cars are reliable.

Now, you may choose to believe what I say or not, and this choice will be affected by whether you think I know what I'm talking about and whether I'm telling the truth. Or not. However, the matter of truth is not likely to give you great pause for thought – why should I lie to you? You're more likely to listen to me and follow my advice if I seem to demonstrate knowledge and experience about the subject of buying second-hand cars, especially if you think that your own knowledge and experience is not equal to mine. You might even (privately) believe that I'm smarter than you, in which case my use of words like 'absolutely' and 'best' will seem natural and completely justified.

So, you may choose to visit the MotorMart where, lo and behold, a 3-year-old white Astra with 44,000 miles on the clock sits invitingly on the forecourt, price £3995. Bearing my advice in mind, you swallow your doubts, negotiate a finance deal with one of the salespeople and drive away in your new possession. Two weeks later the exhaust falls off, the engine seizes up and the doors refuse to close. On your way back from visiting MotorMart, where the owner has just informed you that the fine print in your 6-month Warranty on the car doesn't say anything about replacing exhausts, engines or doors, you bump into me. After you've conveyed the sum and substance of your problems to me in no uncertain terms, you demand an explanation from me – why did I tell you the things I did about Vauxhall Astras? Well, I respond, look around you on any busy street, there are lots of these cars giving years of trouble-free use, how was I to know you'd choose to buy the only one in the city that was a heap of scrap? There isn't any definite answer to that – it was your choice, after all. With an effort, you restrain yourself and walk away. I watch you go, and for a few moments ponder on whether I should perhaps have given you more neutral advice, suggested a range of vehicles maybe, or told you to subscribe to *Which Car?* magazine before making an informed purchase, perhaps refrained from making categorical statements that helped to persuade and convince you that I was the Oracle. Perhaps I should even have told you that I own half of MotorMart in partnership with my uncle. No, perhaps not. I mean, if I had told you all these things, you might not have bought my sales pitch and consequently the car, the profit from which currently lies to my credit in the bank – in company with the commission I got from the finance house who lent you the other £2000.

In the normal course of things, we get used to communicating with each other in ways that we take for granted, and we get to know that different situations require different types of responses from us in the ways that we view and handle our communication with other people. We bring a wide range of perceptions and values and beliefs and habits to the way we exchange information, and departing from the 'norm' of our experiences can be an unsettling business. When, for the first time, you encounter academic literature and find authors writing that:

> The results appear to suggest that the individual consumption of 200 Mars Bars per day might be linked in a cause and effect relationship with an increase in body weight. However, further study is required to investigate this putative relationship, the possible nature of which has been explored in this study but is still far from being fully understood, far less established.

you might be tempted into thinking that any fool knows if you eat too much chocolate you'll end up overweight, and the author is just afraid to commit themselves one way or another, or is just stupid. Which isn't the case at all. The vocabulary and the semantics are not new to you, and the message is plain enough. It's just being presented in a special way, a very careful, cautious way where the overriding emphasis is placed on treating the matter of 'truth' with respect, and never claiming any particle of it without complete justification.

If these issues of being cautious and regarding 'truth' in this respectful light were not followed in the reports of research activity by a strict observance of the rules, the results would grossly ill-serve you and the profession. The reliance we can reasonably place on properly handled and prepared research reports to deal accurately and objectively with their subjects would disappear, and authors would become vendors of information whose easiest reception would lie in the writer's ability to persuade the gullible by subterfuge, rather than convince the critical by reason.

Statistical analysis

One of the tools of scientific investigation is the application of mathematical formulae to numerical data in order to identify, explore and explain the meanings that this data might possess for the investigator.

That sentence would be enough on its own to cause some of us to feel a fair amount of misgiving. Ask us to wade through a research report where numbers are as much in evidence as words and our retreat is complete.

This needn't be the case. The statistical handling of information is part and parcel of a good deal of research activity, and extremely sophisticated mathematics may sometimes be involved in the analysis of data, but the presentation of the results of that analysis in the final paper will not require you to divine and understand every step the numbers took on the way. Instead, the authors will present their numerical data with an explanation of how and why they did what they did and then name the statistical tests and other number-crunching techniques that were used. Certainly, these items themselves might as well be in Sanskrit until you acquire a reasonable grasp of the whole business of statistical analysis. With effort and application that will happen. Not through the medium of these pages, though; I would recommend strongly that you pay close and particular attention to the subject as it is presented in your course and acquire at least two textbooks devoted to the subject, with one of them being, if you're completely unfamiliar with the study of statistics, the most basic primer you can obtain. You might never have to use in earnest all that you learn about statistical analysis, but if you learn enough to be able to understand the import of professional research papers where this type of tool is used, then you'll have spent your time to good purpose.

Taken as a whole, then, research papers are constructed in special ways in order to achieve special purposes. It just takes time and application for you to acquire the skills and experience needed to understand these ways and appreciate the value of the purposes. I've gone on about some characteristics of research publications because it's not unknown for some learners to encounter these reports at an early stage in their professional education, find them difficult to handle, develop a belief that they are impossible to understand, and then avoid them forever more. It's not too wide of the mark to suggest that if we were *all* completely comfortable with the interpretation of research reports, a much wider field of knowledge would be available to the profession.

The messages of research reports can still be grasped by the attentive learner, even though they might be clothed in unfamiliar forms. The point is that these sources of information attempt to convey messages in a medium where no claims are made for 'truth' but a never-ending effort is applied to establishing the appropriate degree of *validity* for what is being said. It is this search for the validity of knowledge that serves the profession best and expands our understanding of what we are, and should be, about as professionals.

EXERCISES

1. Take a three-page sample from each of two textbooks – one should be a basic text, a 'primer', and the other a heavyweight reference book. Make summary notes of each sample as you first read the material. Put these notes to one side.

   Now, read each three-page sample through at least three times. When you think you have a reasonable grasp of the material, write down the main messages, from memory, that you've taken from each text. When these main messages are recorded, go over them and write down any and every detail about them that you can recall.

   Compare these 'remembered' messages with the contents of your summary notes. How do they shape up with each other? What differences exist between the two sets of notes for each sample? You may find that 'remembered' notes are shorter and less detailed than summary notes, but still manage to represent the main textual messages. Go over the texts again with each set of notes to hand and evaluate them in terms of how well they represent the salient points raised in the books.

2. Using these same textbooks, choose a variety of passages from each of them that deals with (a) 'factual' material, (b) specific theory and (c) general concepts or ideas. Note any references which the authors use in these passages and use them to search for the original sources of information. When you've done this, check your selected material against these referenced sources – how has the textbook represented the original information: as a direct quote? by paraphrasing? Do you think that this information is accurately and 'fairly' represented in the book? For example, is anything missing that you think could have been included? Which source of information do you find gives you a better understanding of the material – one or the other? or does reading both give you a fuller picture?

3. Select a subject covered in at least one recent research paper that has also been the topic for discussion in other types of published articles. Gather as many different examples of published work on the subject as

you can, making notes on:

(a) the language used in different articles; and
(b) the amount and nature of any referenced material each author uses,

and try to identify how the perspective which each author places on his or her writing might help or hinder you in:

(a) understanding the material; and
(b) analysing and evaluating the information presented.

4 Essay writing

Essays are required for assessment purposes on most courses, with the result that a lot of learners come to dread them. Which is a pity, because preparing and writing an essay is a valuable learning exercise, and it has the added bonus of earning you credit towards passing your course. Now, I'm not suggesting that essays are easy. They're not; it takes time, effort and skill to produce a good essay; but with practice you can get into the swing of essay writing and accumulate some serious course credit without pain.

MEETING COURSE REQUIREMENTS

A word to the unwary: the word 'Essay' is sometimes subject to abuse by some teachers in some situations. Don't make the assumption that when 'Essays' are mentioned on your course for the first time, you and the teacher are automatically talking about the same thing. The likelihood is that you and the teacher *will* share a common understanding of what an essay is – a piece of written work produced by learners to demonstrate learning, to display skills and abilities in finding, identifying, describing and discussing information; besides which, most courses include instruction on how to meet course requirements for essays, projects and so on.

However, as I noted in Chapter 2, take nothing for granted where course work assessments are concerned. If you're required to submit essays, you have to know what's expected of you. Pore over every scrap of information you're given, and discuss the entire business at length with your teacher or course advisor.

CHOICE OF TOPICS AND 'GIVEN' TOPICS

Essay topics are usually selected by teachers from the contents of the course syllabus, and these topics are then assigned in various ways to the student, the most common of which is either to set a single topic for an entire group, or offer individuals some degree of personal choice of topic from a limited range. Depending on which method is used, there are a few things to keep in mind.

If a single topic is set for your entire group, then the likelihood is that the teacher considers the subject matter important and highly relevant. You should give every essay your best shot, but this is one to be very particular about. Remember too that if everyone else is handing in an essay on the same topic, you have to make an extra effort with yours: even the most saintly of good teachers gets a bit disenchanted wading through 20 or more essays on the same subject – it might be necessary, but it isn't fun. This is not the time to hand over a pile of scrappy waffle.

Any choice of topic is a gift, so use it sensibly. The most obvious criteria to use in making your choice are those of interest, knowledge and value. If you're already interested in the topic, you've cracked it. If you already have some knowledge in the subject, wonderful. If the topic has an obvious value (as a subject in previous exams, perhaps?), go for it; but be cautious. Consider the list very carefully, weigh up the choices as best you can, discuss them with your teacher.

SUBJECT/FORMAT/LENGTH

Most teachers prepare handouts about essays which list the topics and give a breakdown on how the essay should be prepared. If the information you receive on essay preparation is clear and unequivocal, all well and good – follow it to the letter. If it's unclear, or not detailed enough, or if you are left in *any* doubt about what's required of you, go forth and get it straightened out, make very sure that you know exactly what is expected of you, and stick to it. Most teachers will be happy to discuss things like this with you since it's likely to save you both a lot of time and effort.

With the proviso that any local expectations made of essay writing are binding on you as a learner on the course, the information given below might round out some important points and steer you in the right direction.

Subject

Read the topic description with great care before you do any preparation. It's all too easy to go off collecting material and writing screeds of good stuff only to discover, usually when it's too late, that you've missed the whole point of the topic. So read it over, ponder the subject, get it straight, consider it well, engrave it on your brain. Every move you make on preparing and writing an essay is guided by the subject, and it's a lot easier to make the effort when you know exactly what you're doing.

Format

Essays, as written material to be assessed, should be as 'reader-friendly' as you can make them. If you haven't read about 'legibility' in Chapter 2, do it now.

Now, so far as the *appearance* of the essay is concerned, whether it's handwritten, typewritten or printed from a PC, some general rules can be followed.

1. Include a Title Page – that is, a covering page that is blank except for the following items of information:
   the essay title
   your name
   the title of the course you're attending
   the name of the educational institution
2. Write on one side of the paper only, leaving margins of at least 3–4 cm *all* around the text.
3. 'References' and 'Bibliography' information should be written on separate pages which follow the last page of the essay.

There is no abstruse and elevated reason for doing all this; it's simply for neatness and readability. Give yourself every chance to make the message come across with great clarity.

Length

Essay lengths are usually given in the number of words you are expected to write, so that you'll be asked to submit essays of 1500 words, or 5000 words, or whatever. Fix this number in your brain in extremely short order and do not forget it. The word length of essays serves a number of purposes. Contrary to what you might suspect, the very least of these purposes is to limit the amount of material the teacher has to slog through.

Word-lengths are good indicators of the amount of work you will be expected to do in terms of preparation. Now, this notion catches some people out, since they presume that the shorter the essay is to be, the lighter will be the workload in preparing it. This is not the case. A short essay on a big subject can be more problematic than a 5000-word essay on some teeny-weeny subject that no one knows very much about.

As a very general rule, a 'comparison' between the expected word-length of an essay and the size of the topic to be covered, can give you a fairly accurate notion of just how to deal with the subject. Obviously, if you're asked to write a 750-word essay on The History of Nursing, you're not going to spend time rooting out the obscure details of every milestone in professional history; you don't have the space. On the other side of the coin, dealing with Professional Accountability in Nursing Practice in 5000 words would give you lots of elbow room to go into the matter in depth.

Always do your level best to stick to a word-length that you're given. Don't submit skinny little efforts when you've been asked for a biggie, and never be tempted to smack down the equivalent of *War and Peace* on your teacher's desk when they're expecting two pages of A4. The maximum freedom you should allow yourself in hitting the target length is 10 per cent of the total, either way. One thing you have to watch out for, especially if you're new to this essay business, is the hot surge of deranged enthusiasm that drives you to attempt writing the best essay the teacher has ever read. In virtually every case of this kind, 'best' means 'longest', and the result is that a piddling little essay that should have taken you a few days to put together assumes the proportions of a PhD thesis. 'Best' essays have a nasty habit of souring their writer's happiness, because their reception is usually very poor indeed. So, stick to what you're asked to do. I'm not saying don't make special efforts, but you must always be sure to channel your energy correctly, and writing essays that belong in three volumes is a non-starter.

I'll return to the subject of 'best' essays later, under the heading 'Drafting and Redrafting'.

THE USE OF REFERENCES

Don't look away, come back here. You're going to have to come to grips with this subject sooner or later, and this section is a painless little introduction to it, a little taster of what it's all about. More detail on this topic is given in the following chapter on Literature Reviews, but I make no apologies for spreading the subject around a bit.

In this context, a 'reference' is made when a writer identifies a piece of information they have used as being borrowed from another writer's work. At its simplest level, the use of references ensures that recognition is given to the person or persons from whom the present writer has learned something. Further, this recognition is given in a particular way, so that readers may check the original source of information for themselves.

References can be made to any written material, published or unpublished, which a writer has used in the preparation of his or her own work, and the reference system that's used must supply the reader with enough information to enable the reader to identify which bits of information are associated with which writers. In addition, the reader must be told where that information can be found. There are two referencing systems in common use, and I'll give you examples of these below. A word of caution first – you will no doubt discover that the staff of your educational institution have a favourite referencing system. Use it. And never employ two different systems in one piece of work.

The Harvard System

Here, a piece of information 'borrowed' by the writer from someone else is identified in the text by naming the original author or authors and giving the date of the original publication. The way in which names and dates are given depends upon which *style* of writing is used. For example, making a direct quote:

> . . . as McMahon & Winters (1992) have noted – 'Audits for external Accreditation of Health Services should be professionally led'.

or when paraphrasing:

> . . . such as the issue of professional leadership in conducting Audits of Health Services which are concerned with external Accreditation (McMahon & Winters, 1992).

You can see that the placing of names and dates and the presence or absence of parentheses is decided by the way in which information is presented, and with practice you soon get to know what goes where. The main point to remember is to make sure you link the piece of information as closely as possible with the name or names, and that the date follows immediately afterwards.

The source of each and every piece of information that you use in the text in this way *must* be given to the reader at the end of your essay, and included on a separate page entitled 'References'. There is a strict rule about this list: you must give *all* of the information necessary about the source of the referenced material so that a reader can track it down personally, so that the reader can, in effect, check up on what you've been saying; they can see for themselves whether you've quoted other authors accurately and used their material correctly. Or not. As the case may be.

There are a number of things to be careful of when putting a 'References' page together, and the content of each entry will vary slightly depending on whether you're using information from a journal article, a book, or a chapter taken from a book where different authors write different sections. I'll cover these points from a general standpoint first, and then detail how the different sources of material affect the result.

Author's name   The author's name always comes first in any reference, with the surname written in full and in capital letters. Then comes the initial letter of the forename. Make sure you spell the name correctly, and include the initial letter of every forename noted for the author, for example:

DAVIES B.L.

Being accurate here is important. If you record these details wrongly, someone might spend wasted time chasing a reference for a non-existent author in an index, looking for DAVIS D. or DAVEYS T.

If more than one author is responsible for the material you must list every name that's noted on the original source, and these must be given in the order in which they appear:

SCROOGE E., SYKES B., DODGER A.

You get the picture. When you do find these pieces written by a group of people, the first name given is that of the acknowledged 'principal author' and this name must always appear when the piece is used for a reference. In the text of an essay, or whatever, though, there is no need to quote everybody's name; the short Latin phrase 'et al.' is used to indicate that other people were involved:

. . . and times were very hard (Scrooge *et al.*, 1879).

'And others' is a direct translation of '*et al.*', so don't get carried away and use it when only two authors are involved, when it is more appropriate to quote both names.

Date   The date is given directly after the last named author (in brackets).

HOOD R., MARION M. (1990)

Order   In the Harvard system, references are listed alphabetically, so that the reader may easily find particular items, no matter where the information they're interested in has appeared in the text. Make sure your list is in correct alphabetical order; check it over. I know this sounds simplistic, but disordered lists are all too easy to produce.

Journal articles

Once the name(s) and date have been noted, the next thing to appear is the full title of the journal article from which the information was taken:

> SMITH J.D. (1987) Conceptual models of nursing care; uses and abuses in daily practice.

Sometimes, these titles can be long and complicated, dotted with hyphens, colons and semi-colons, capital letters, numbers, acronyms and so on. Reproduce all of it faithfully, because it's that author's title, not yours. Put it down exactly as you found it.

The next thing you have to do is to identify the journal in which the article appeared, and this must be the full title by which it is registered as a publication:

> SMITH J.D. (1987) Conceptual models of nursing care; uses and abuses in daily practice. *The Duty Room Weekly*

The exact issue of the journal must be specified, which involves noting the *Volume* number and the *Issue* number (the 'part' of the Volume). Lastly, you must note the number of the page or pages on which the article appeared:

> SMITH J.D. (1987) Conceptual models of nursing care; uses and abuses in daily practice. *The Duty Room Weekly* 5, 2, 19–23.

These details must be given as fully as possible, since they can lead the reader directly to the source material without fuss or bother.

Books

After the author's name and date have been noted, next comes the title of the book, written just as it would appear for an article. Following this is the publisher's name and the place of publication:

ARGYLL D., SUTHERLAND T.Q. (1973) A philosophy of nursing care. Whyte and Mackay, London.

This information can be found on the first page or two of the book.

Now, in making reference to a book, you can leave the reference list entry just as it stands here, and it's quite legitimate for you to do so. What you might find, however, is that teachers sometimes like to have a book reference made a little more specific, especially if you've used direct quotes from the text. In this case, you may note chapter and page numbers (or even just page numbers) and insert these after the book title.

The only other difference that might be made in the book reference occurs when a book is published and then undergoes successive *editions*. This means that the original text has been changed to some degree; a second edition is not the exact same book as the first edition, it is not a straightforward *reprinting* of the original text. What this means is that if a book has undergone several editions (revisions by the author or others) you must indicate from which edition you took the information you used, so that the reader is made aware of this. You can imagine that situations could arise where your information comes from the third edition of a book but on searching for it the reader obtains a copy of the first edition, which doesn't contain the information you've worked from; or the information is there somewhere, but it's on a different page.

So, if different editions of a book have been published, indicate the one you have used in your reference:

ARGYLL D., SUTHERLAND T.Q. (1987) A philosophy of nursing care. (3rd Edn) Whyte & Mackay, London.

A chapter taken from a book

In this instance, you've used material by an author who has contributed a chapter to someone else's book, so you have to note two sets of titles and authors for the reader. It's straightforward enough, though; you note the author and date and title of the chapter, and then indicate where it is to be found and who produced the book:

WORTHY A. (1991) Patient satisfaction surveys. In Quality assurance and nursing care, Louise Rose & William Chianti (Eds) Lamb & Brusco, Edinburgh.

Again, this form of reference is capable of standing on its own; you've given the reader enough information to track it down. Remember that you might be asked to give more detail, in which case insert the first and last page numbers of the chapter.

The Vancouver System

The main difference between this system and the Harvard system is that information points to your text are not just named, they are *numbered*. That is, the material you wish to reference is identified by the insertion of a number, and this number corresponds with the reference list, where the usual full details of the original source are given. The numbers are usually inserted into the text in one of two ways, either in brackets or by lifting them slightly above the level of the line of text:

> . . . but a recent study has noted that nurse learners rarely eat junk food (6)

> . . . although it can be argued that the phrase 'junk food' means different things to different people[7].

Sometimes, you may find that a point of information can be referenced by noting two or more sources of material. In this case, more than one reference number can be inserted at the appropriate spot in the text.

The reference list is made up in *numerical* order, with the original sources noted and described following the sequence in which they appeared in the text. If you refer to the same work twice or more in any text, always use the first number that you assigned to it.

> **1.** POST E., SMITH S. (1985) . . . and continue the remainder of the reference details here, as you would with the Harvard system.

And that's it for now on using references. There is more to follow in the next chapter, so I'll content myself here with a few cautionary words of advice to sum up this bit:

- Use the referencing system required on your course.
- Make sure your references are as accurate as possible.
- Always check over your reference list to make sure it is in perfect order.

And please, don't waste a second on worrying about the length of any reference list you might compile in the course of writing an essay. A single appropriate and well-placed reference can be worth dozens of useless references shovelled in to pad out a poor piece of work. Once you've had practice in reading and writing referenced 'academic' material, you'll soon see how easy it is to spot the difference, and you can bet your boots your teachers are well aware of what to look for.

Okay, you've got your topic, you know exactly what's required of you in writing your essay, and you've some idea of what references are and how they should be used. What's next? Information-gathering.

INFORMATION POOL

The easiest mistake to make in writing an essay is to assume that you know something about the subject well enough to start writing without checking that what you 'know' is neither imagination nor fabrication.

The point is that, like it or not, you're about to prepare an academic paper for someone to read, and this someone will assess the contents using a number of criteria, not least important of which are accuracy of information and the context in which it is presented.

That sounds a bit grim, but it can be boiled down to two things – *background* and *details*, the two most useful factors in determining your approach to the essay construction.

READING, READING AND MORE READING

The better you understand the essay topic, then the easier this bit will be. Most topics can point you towards a mountain of information, so you have to narrow the approach down as much as possible, and a clear understanding of the topic is your best starting point.

Now is the time for you to become closely acquainted with the contents of your favourite library, and to start the serious application of all the stuff we talked about in Chapter 2 under 'Reading'. You're about to start sharpening up some vital skills in finding and using information.

First of all, identify what you consider to be the main subject covered by the essay topic, and go for the broadest-based material about it that you can lay your hands on. What you're looking for is a general perspective on the subject; you want to know something of it and become familiar with it without delving into too much detail at this stage. Textbooks are your best bet for this, since they are meant to be instructive and explanatory, and usually present the kind of wider picture that you're looking for. It might be that your subject isn't contained in any textbooks because it's very new in the field, or for some reason it barely rates a mention in most texts. Fair enough, look elsewhere if you must, but cover the textbook ground as thoroughly as you can first.

Once you have some grasp of the information surrounding a subject, you can begin to elicit more detail about it from sources other than textbooks. This is where you make a beeline for the professional journals, and start to track down specific points, creating a knowledge base for yourself.

Journal articles which describe and discuss other published material on a specific subject are called 'Literature Reviews', and these can be of the greatest value to you. They not only pull together lots of information from many sources into the kind of 'digest' which increases your awareness of the subject, but the best of them are beautifully balanced presentations which look at the subject from differing points of view. One good literature review can open your eyes to a world of information, a particularly helpful aspect of which is that the reference list is likely to be both extensive and comprehensive. These lists can be a goldmine for you, saving an immense amount of time in chasing relevant material.

Other types of journal articles should also be looked for, and these may be research-based papers, commentaries by experts or general 'feature' articles. The reference lists that might accompany any of these types of presentation should be checked over, but the likelihood is that only the research-based papers will provide you with new avenues to follow.

Depending on the topic, it might be the case that information about the subject will be contained in written sources other than textbooks and journals, such as HMSO publications, or Local Health Authority reports. This is when good librarians come into their own, and start putting you in front of material you might never find for yourself without disappearing among the shelves for long and weary searches. Always draw on the help of an expert when you can.

So, the story this far: you've been acquiring information and getting acquainted with it, delving into the subject and cranking up your knowledge level, digging a pit (as it were) and filling it with a flow of data. However, how are you to stop this pool of information from just draining away again? Very simply, start handling the information, and the easiest way to do this is by preparing Essay Notes.

Note-taking has already been discussed in Chapter 2, and the general principles discussed then with regard to being concise and precise apply here, and vitally so. Writing an 'academic' paper such as an essay requires you to pay close attention to detail, and shoddy notes will not serve you well. However, that said, there are differences between 'ordinary' notes and essay notes.

ESSAY NOTES

Essay notes are notes for an essay, like the preliminary sketches an artist would make who intended to produce a full-blown portrait in oils. These notes are the bare bones, the skeleton of the eventual essay.

The point is that since a good essay displays an understanding of the topic, it is never too early to begin an attempt at acquiring that understanding. In essay notes there is a kernel of acquired information, surrounded by a pertinent shell of related comments. No matter if this shell is just one comment thick, or even one thick comment, it requires you to think about the information you're acquiring, to begin to consider the subject you'll be writing about. Essentially, the message here is that it's never too early to think.

Before going on to laying out how essay notes are constructed, I want to say a word or two about writing 'style' in essays: unless you've been directly instructed to present your essay in an informal 'first person' style, it's usually best to adopt a more formal approach. There are two main aspects to this 'academic' style, both of which are designed to introduce a certain 'tone' to your writing.

(a)   Don't make a personal appearance in your essay. The most common advice given at this time is for you to write in the 'third person' – which is fair enough, and means that if you feel you absolutely *have* to mention yourself and your personal experiences, then you phrase it in a certain way. For example:

> '. . . but no information of this kind was discovered by the author . . .'

> '. . . although, in the writer's experience, nursing is not an unemotional activity . . .'

The 'author' or 'writer' is of course you, and there are times when you might want to insert yourself into the text, but it can be a very sticky practice to begin and an absolute quagmire to escape.

It is much simpler to stay invisible and make no personal references whatsoever. Now, you may be unused to writing like this, but it's only another habit you have to acquire. Read through textbooks and research-based articles and you'll soon pick up on that neutral tone.

What you might find helpful is to imagine that between you and your reader is a detached, disinterested observer who is willing to pass on any messages you give them, but in doing so will remove all trace of personal involvement. Essentially, this 'third person' would act as a reporter, but would transmit messages stripped of any obvious subjectivity. This point is the primary reason for the 'academic' writing style: you are required to learn *objectivity* in handling information – in the way you receive it, in the way you process it, and in the way you transmit it.

(b) Don't appear dogmatic, didactic or dictatorial. The point is that you're writing the essay as a learner, not as an expert. If you write as though you have absolute knowledge and claim absolute 'truth' for what you're saying, then you're in serious bother if the reader knows differently and can prove you wrong. For example, instead of phrases such as:

'. . . Research in the field has proved that nurses are often able to communicate with a patient when everyone else has failed to do so . . .'

where you're taking terrible risks with the 'facts', take care not to overstep the mark. A sensible person might write:

'. . . Some studies have shown that . . .'

or:

'. . . From these findings it might be suggested that . . .'

The vital point here is *accuracy*, and you must attempt to demonstrate your intention to handle information with a respect for strict accuracy.

It's all too easy to get bogged down on 'style' and aggravate yourself into indignation because you don't see why you should have to write in a certain way. Since the 'style' is essentially concerned with trying to achieve *objectivity* and *accuracy*, you really don't have much room to manoeuvre. Like any other human activity, the writing of academic papers can occur on a scale which goes from the sublime to the ridiculous. Try to become comfortable with writing in a simple, straightforward way that relates information clearly, accurately and without bias.

Now, you're ready to begin writing your essay notes, and you can prepare these in three stages: Gathering and Selecting, Writing and Relating and Grouping and Linking.

Gathering and Selecting

With your essay topic right at the forefront of your consciousness, pasted on the inside of your forehead, gather together all of the information you've collected and start sifting through it, looking for material that should be included in the essay.

This is a glib thing to say, but with an understanding of your topic you should be able to work out what the boundaries of your essay should be, and having *read and considered* your information pool, you should be in a position to discriminate between what you can use and what you can shelve. If you find yourself completely unable to tell the difference between what you can use and what you can't, then you've probably not read and considered enough. You can only start selecting relevant material when you are sufficiently acquainted with what it means. You don't have to understand everything with stunning clarity, but you must have got in among the material and be familiar with the messages contained there. Essentially, you're fishing in the information pool with a net you've sewn together as a result of your reading, and the efficiency of that net will be in direct proportion to the amount of effort you have *already* made.

When you're sifting through your information, start making notes on points you wish to retain. For each point, carefully record the details of its origin; you may wish to make use of this information as reference material when you come to write the essay.

Writing and Relating

When you're satisfied that you've dredged all you can from your information pool, you can start to knock your rough notes into some kind of order. A simple way to do this is to prepare a Card Index system.

Get yourself a stock of 8 × 4 in lined cards. You can use loose sheets of paper, but it's easier to stack and handle cards, and you'll be using them a lot. Now:

1. Read through your notes with great care and highlight points which relate to each other, which are connected in some way.
2. Transfer groups of these related points on to your cards, noting all the details about the origin of each point.

   This 'grouping' of points can be done simply by limiting the number of points on each card, but have a stab at trying to make each group a little network of *closely related* information.
3. Where individual points of information remain on your notes, transfer all of these onto single cards until all of your original notes have been transcribed onto your card system.

   These individual points might be a single item of general information, a quote, a statistic, or some 'historical' fact.

When you're preparing these cards, it's important for you to keep an open mind on what you've seen fit to record in your original notes – BUT, as you go through them, you might find that by avoiding duplication and trimming untidy prose, you can cut your material down somewhat. This is all right, exercise a bit of judgment by all means, especially if you're an inveterate and indiscriminate note-taker with volumes of dog-eared pages at your elbow. However, the transfer of information to your cards shouldn't be a complete rewrite.

Grouping and Linking

The aim of this stage is to place your cards in a sensible running order, one that tells the tale required of your essay. There are a number of ways to do this, some of them easier than others, but all of them revolve around finding and developing *themes* and placing information in *context*.

Theme(s)

A 'theme' is any idea or topic upon which you would expand in your essay. Themes can be big or small; you might find that a short essay allows for the identification and development of just one theme. On the other hand, and depending on the subject, a lengthy essay may require you to expand upon a number of ideas or topics.

The selection of themes for an essay can be made by going through your card system and grouping together those cards which deal with the same topic. If you find that all of your cards do so – fine, you have a single theme. More often, you're likely to find some differences between items that require you to identify several themes, several 'strands' to your essay, each of which you wish to discuss and expand upon. That's fine, too. Don't worry about having little islands of cards lying about, it's important for you to recognise that your essay may be made of various 'bits' which you will weld together.

Context

'Context' describes the parts of a piece of writing that go before or follow after a word or passage, and which contribute to its full meaning. If, for example, you read the sentence '. . . with a large bill . . .' on its own, what are you to make of it? Very little, since you have no context within which to fit it, except in a very general sense – you recognise the words and they convey something to you, but while they contain information, they are not informative in that no message is transmitted. By the addition of further information, preceding and following the statement, a message is created – 'She refused to lend me a penny since, with a large bill outstanding, I was a very poor credit risk'. So, now we know this large bill has nothing to do with ducks, that it concerns me, the actions of myself and another person, and something of my past history. The message comes out of the statement when it's put into context; its meaning is made clearer.

This is all very well, you've known about context for years; but it's often the case that people writing essays – bright, articulate, earnest people – forget all about it and put together messages so wobbly and unconnected they're in danger of falling off the page.

Handling the context of an essay is easy IF you're familiar with the information it will contain. In other words, you have to know what you're writing about. I'm sorry, but it's the only way. It doesn't matter how brilliantly you might write, ignorance in the brain won't beget sense on the page. If you can't connect up the message, how can the reader be expected to do so?

With 'themes' and 'context' as the signposts, you should be able to help the reader find a path through your essay. No one should be left to flounder around in a morass of disconnected data. Messages shouldn't take readers by surprise; they should be led up to, rounded out, explained.

WRITING FOR A READER

There are only two legitimate assumptions you can make about the person who will read and assess your essay: first, they are intelligent, and second, they know what you're supposed to be writing about. That's it. It's hard enough to write with simplicity and clarity without confusing yourself with all kinds of value judgments about how bright the assessor is or how much they might know about the essay topic. Your essay isn't a test of an assessor's intelligence; it's meant to display your skills and abilities.

It can be very tempting to assume that readers will be so quick on the uptake that they will 'fill in' for themselves those nasty little gaps with which your essay is peppered, or that they will know enough about the topic so that your omission of all that boring background material won't matter. Please don't kid yourself. The essay format in course assessment is meant to showcase your capacity to learn and communicate, to acquire and handle information that is of value to you.

Recognising that you don't have to pitch the essay at some imaginary level for the reader leaves you free to get on with describing, explaining and discussing your material as best you can. There, in those three words of 'describe, explain, discuss', are the tools with which you can start to piece your essay together. Writing an essay is not some monumentally creative task that you'll never accomplish; all you have to do is describe your information, explain what it means and then discuss it sensibly and without fuss.

Does that sound too easy? But what more is there? If you can do these three things with every item of information you introduce then you will be demonstrating competence of a very high order. Certainly, as you progress in your learning you might be required to handle more detailed, more complex, perhaps more abstract information, but the basic expectations made of you will be the same – how well do you handle information?

NARRATIVE FLOW

This is a fancy title, which sums up what a good essay should do: it should tell a story smoothly. Not brilliantly, not perfectly, it doesn't need to read like Shakespeare. All that's required is that it should be readable and informative.

Some of the topics you'll find in this section have been touched on in Chapter 2, and they are dealt with in a bit more detail here.

With your card index in order, your issues identified and some comments made, you already have the framework of your essay and an approximate idea of how items will fit into the context of the finished work. So, the time has finally come to pick up your pen (or take the cover off the typewriter or switch on the PC) and write.

Not everybody sits down to write an essay from the first sentence to the last, in one session. Lots of people take days (or even weeks) to piece together an essay; and lots of people write bits of the middle first, then the end, and then the beginning. It all depends on what you're comfortable with. Try this:

1. Have a look at your cards – could any part of the essay framework be split into sections? Parts of an essay can be worked on separately and then connected up with the rest of the text, there's no law that says it can't be done.
2. What's the strongest point that you will make in the essay? Pick it out and have a go at writing it down in full. When you've done that, write another two sentences – the first sentence should connect the point with what precedes it in your framework, the second should lead on to the next point to be made.
3. Is there a point or a set of points that you feel most comfortable with in

your cards? Choose one or all of them and write down whatever you want to say.

4. Which bit of your framework gives you the heebie-jeebies? Look it square in the face and write about it. Get it down on paper, put it into words and sentences.

You see, the trick is to start writing, because when you do, you take command of the situation and you can do what you will. If you drag your feet and put it off, it will become harder and harder to begin, and a little essay will slowly assume gargantuan proportions and deceive you into believing they require a monumental effort to accomplish. Once you put pen to paper and make a start, you're in charge, the Encyclopaedia Brittanica shrinks back to 800 words and the hollow pit of your stomach begins to fill with a warm glow of righteousness. Okay, so your first attempts won't be perfect, so what? Keep trying.

The thing that most people worry about is not the points they will make but how they will knit them together. That's fair enough, your essay should read well; but it doesn't have to be seamless. Bear in mind that as a narrative, the only requirement made of your essay is that a reader should be able to follow your line of thought as it appears on the page. If you're gifted at knitting yarns, all well and good. If you're not, the few tips given below might help.

Point by Point

Concentrate first on describing each point that you must make when you first bring it up in the essay. Be plain before you get fancy. If you go on to combine two or more points you'll make much more sense if you've already told the reader what each of them is. Making associations between different bits of material forms the greater part of a lot of essays, and most people tie themselves in knots trying to describe individual items and at the same time explain their associations.

Points and Paragraphs

Each sentence should have a point to it, whether it's an item of specific information or a general comment. Don't waste your time on trying to craft beautiful little links between bits of data. Say something that has meaning or say nothing.

Use paragraphs to focus the reader's attention and help them through the essay. The shorter the better is a good rule of thumb. Sometimes, you might find it impossible to break with one paragraph and go on to another, but this usually occurs either because (a) you've clustered too many points of information together, or (b) you're worrying about those little links again. Reducing the number of points dealt with will solve (a) and as for (b) – don't bother, just get on with it.

First and Last Paragraphs

Both of these paragraphs are included in the word count of an essay, so don't waste them; make sure they work for you. The first should briefly say what the essay is about, the last should bring the essay to a stop.

First paragraphs are easy: 'This paper is about the care of elderly people living in long-stay hospital wards, and the possible influences that nurses might have on the physical health of these individuals'. That's it. Your intention is to plant the first message into the mind of the reader as quickly as you can and fix it there. Be brief, blunt and bold. The reader shouldn't be half-way down the second page before they find out what you're going to say.

Last paragraphs can either be easy or a disaster, so they need a bit of thought. The only hard and fast rule to observe here is that you should never introduce new information at the end of the essay. Don't spring any surprises on the reader, don't annoy them by starting to pull rabbits from hats just when they thought the curtain was coming down.

Last paragraphs should be very much to the point and should be (if you can possibly manage it) a distillation of the main message, or messages, of the essay. I'll be frank with you; this is much easier said than done, and often depends more on the type of material you're dealing with than on anything else. You might find it more practical to use a last paragraph as a means of putting some perspective on the subject. For example:

> The lack of agreement between researchers in this field suggests that further studies are required. The issue of whether or not certain types of nursing care can bring about physical dependency in patients is too important to be left undecided.

Keep it as simple as you can. It can be a great temptation to 'sign off ' with a flourish, and let your relief at finishing an essay push you into grandiose nonsense. Guard against it. Go out on a firm, quiet note.

Now, it's too much to expect that tidy, well-constructed first and last paragraphs can rescue a poor essay from the bin. However, they can make an impression and leave an impression on the reader, so it's worth spending some time and effort on them.

Muddling the Middle Bit

The bit that falls between the first and last paragraphs of an essay can either be a lucid stream of information or a great uncharted ocean of disconnected data. Which will yours be? I'm going to give you two guidelines to follow which you will read, mark and inwardly digest. Then you will go on to the next section, where the bad news awaits.

1. The key to lucidity is clarity.
2. The key to clarity is simplicity.

Drafting and redrafting

Very, very few people can write accurately enough to say what they want to say first time, every time. By far the majority of us need to make a few attempts to get the message straight. Even when we do try to make ourselves understood on paper, there sits upon our shoulder the demon Conceit, who makes us use 10 words where one would do and whispers unholy jargon in our ears. So throw some salt over your shoulder, get out a large supply of paper, and get ready to write.

First draft

With your card index in order, lift one card at a time and write down, in sensible language, each point recorded there with your comments. Add whatever details or further remarks you wish, but delete nothing. Don't worry about how it looks, just get it down. When the last card has been used, tack on a first and last paragraph.

Now, read it through and check that you have faithfully copied all the details on the cards as they appear. Take great care with this, since you will not refer to the cards again, unless it is to construct a reference list.

Read it through again, this time to see if it makes any sense at all, correct obvious mistakes, such as duplications and spelling errors, and add any material that occurs to you. Delete nothing.

Second draft

With your first draft in front of you, write the whole thing out again. This time, read each sentence over three or four times, decide upon the exact meaning of what you want that sentence to convey, and then remove any and every word or phrase that you can remove without affecting the meaning of the sentence. If you believe you cannot remove so much as a single word, then try replacing any big words with smaller words. When you're convinced that a sentence is as trim, clear and concise as you can make it, write it into the second draft. When this is finished, read it through.

In this latest reading, concentrate on the subject matter of individual paragraphs – is each point, each bit of information in context? If not, can whole sentences be switched around to make it so? Can parts of different sentences be welded together, or would the addition of a new sentence make the paragraph work? Is there a rogue sentence in there which is serving to confuse the issue: if so, does it belong somewhere else, or can it be deleted altogether? When you're satisfied that each paragraph is made up of sentences in context, read the whole thing through again. Several times.

What you're looking for now is how paragraphs fit into the overall context of the essay. Are messages started and finished, or left hanging in mid-air? Are connections made briefly, and are they relevant? Would any reordering of paragraphs make your message clearer, could connections be made shorter, could associations be made more definite?

Once you're satisfied that both sentences and paragraphs are in context, check the word length. You can count each word, or make an approximation. If the total is within 90–110 per cent of the given length of the essay, breathe a sigh of relief. If it's drastically short or way over the top, you have to do something about it.

Short of the mark   Leave the second draft as it is and go back to the drawing board. You need more information. Use the card index for clues to acquiring more data, read around your subject more, chase down those references you might have ignored the first time around. Construct more cards with new information, handled in the same way as before, and see if you can't insert these items *appropriately* into the second draft. Whatever you do, listen very carefully; whatever you do, don't pad out a short essay with long strings of rambling waffle. If you're really stuck for time, and you can't get near the expected word total, go on to the third draft stage but make sure your teacher or course leader knows what's happening.

Way over the top   Reduce it. You've written too much, and it doesn't matter whether you've just been too enthusiastic in your data collection or whether there are a lot of unnecessary passages in the text. Something's got to go. Read over the next section with great care and remember, the word lengths of essays are set for good reasons – bigger doesn't always mean better.

Third draft

It's time to write the fair copy that will be handed in as your essay. By this time you've written it out at least twice, and read it through half-a-dozen times or more. This can be a tiresome, tedious business and it's easy to let your attention wander, but it all pays off, it's worth making the effort. You know this essay now, you understand the material, you've pieced it together and learned a lot on the way.

Okay, whether you're using pen, typewriter or PC, think clean and tidy; use fresh paper, good pen, ribbon or cartridge, and take your time. Go through the final version of the second draft with a ruthless disregard for your feelings, let nothing by you that doesn't make sense, simplify and clarify everything that needs it. Don't rush, don't get annoyed with yourself, slow down and concentrate on making your messages as plain and straightforward as you can.

When you're finished, take a break. If time allows, let the essay sit for a day, and then read it over. If an obvious mistake or absurdity jumps off the page at you, correct it. Otherwise, don't be tempted just to fiddle with minor points, it is possible to over-polish a text and fall into the bottomless pit of perfection, whose walls are so smooth you can never climb out. Be satisfied with an honest attempt at clarity; there will be other essays to do, you can't spend your life on just one of them.

Now, put everything in order – title page, numbered pages of text, reference list and bibliography – whatever's required, and fasten it all together. Insert it into a clean, waterproof cover if that is your earnest wish and submit it.

EXERCISES

1. Get hold of a list of essay topics that have been used on your course in the recent past, and choose two of them to work with – one that you're interested in and know something about, and one that, given a choice, you normally wouldn't touch with a barge-pole. Start reading around both subjects and try to identify at least two strong themes for each of them, then have a go at developing these themes in writing. Set yourself a maximum of 400 words for each attempt. Persuade a teacher to read them through and make comments on them.
2. Find out which referencing system your course leader prefers you to use, pick a subject for investigation, then start using your library to collect data on it. Choose information from a mixture of books and journals, and from each of these pick one or two points of information.

Write sentences that include this borrowed information, construct paragraphs in which you insert several references. When each item has been used, make up a reference list, and then have someone read the whole piece over for accuracy.

3. Practise writing first and last paragraphs for essays on subjects you know well. Or try rewriting the first and last paragraphs of articles in professional journals – can you make their message simpler, more clear?

4. Check through the procedure given in Chapter 3 for discovering the Fog Index of any text, and then apply it to samples of your own writing.

    (a) Whatever the results might be, try simplifying the messages in your text so that it still says what you want it to say, but the Fog Index drops by at least 2.

    (b) If any result is 18 or more, rewrite the text until the Index drops below this figure. The original message must still be intact.

5 Literature reviews

Where a course requires you to complete one or more Literature Reviews, the likelihood is that the results will form an important component of the overall assessment strategy used to investigate your learning. For that reason alone you should give them careful attention. However, there is an even better reason: compiling a Literature Review is an exacting academic task that brings you nose to nose with salient material that forms the body of knowledge your course needs you to acquire. There is no better way to become intimately acquainted with what you need to know as a learner in a profession – not only in terms of essential information, but also with regard to how you acquire that information and what you will do with it.

First, a definition is in order: a 'Literature Review' is a written piece of work that attempts to identify significant past and current thinking on a particular topic, reduce it to a manageable size while maintaining accuracy and exploring the relationships one piece of information may have with others, and present it in as logical a form as possible – with or without discussion.

There we are. Clear as mud. We'll try again: a 'Literature Review' is *not* an Essay, or a Project Report, Commentary or Case Study. It *is* the result of a comprehensive and exhaustive search through the literature available on any given topic, performed in order to equip the writer (and the reader) with an accurate digest of relevant information that remains pertinent to the subject of interest.

A bit better. It got away at the end though. Once more: a 'Literature Review' is a learning exercise which your teachers will set you with four aims in mind:

1. to increase your knowledge about the subject of the Review;
2. to put you in the position of using and honing skills in the acquisition of information;

3. to give you practice in analysing and evaluating information, and to encourage the development of critical thinking; and
4. to prepare you for conducting research activity.

That seems to encompass it fairly well. I've told you three times now what I believe a Literature Review is. It's up to you to find out whether your course organisers have anything else to add. Which they just might – Literature Reviews and the learning you will undergo in handling them are central to your development of an academic expertise; your teachers may well wish to underscore this development by making some 'special' requirements mandatory in completing a Review. Discover what these are and stick closely to them.

A Review, like any piece of written work, begins with the selection of a topic. Here, we can consider this selection in two ways.

1. Where the topic is preselected on your behalf by a teacher, who assigns it to you with a specific purpose in mind. This purpose might be made up of a number of reasons, but one of them will most likely be drawn from the intention that you will 'teach yourself' about a specific subject rather than have it presented to you in a lecture.
2. Where you are given the opportunity to select a topic personally, usually with certain boundaries set on the subject matter. Again though, you may find that the material you deal with in the Review is not, or only partially, 'covered' in other ways in the course.

This use of the Review as a 'self-teaching' instrument is deliberately aimed at encouraging you to think *and* act for yourself as a learner, with the target of *independent* learning firmly in mind.

As always, consider the topic with care, establish it clearly as a message with meaning and use it as a signpost for directing your efforts. You might find that while explanatory texts you receive from your teachers on how to construct the Review are fully detailed (read them with care, pay close attention, do what they ask) the topics themselves are little more than brief titles. For example:

> *'The practical application of nursing audit'*
> *'Post-operative analgesia'*
> *'Information technology in nursing'*

Since the field of knowledge represented might be huge, these 'catch-all' titles can be a little scary. Don't be put off; comprehensive and exhaustive enquiry is one thing – the expected length of the finished review is another. The best parameters to apply in understanding the topic and how it will be translated into the eventual Review are best determined in discussion with your teacher. If you don't have clear guidelines on the expected breadth and depth of the Review, sort these issues out with the teacher on two occasions: (a) when you're first presented with the task, and (b) after you've become fairly well acquainted with the relevant available literature. The first discussion will set you on your way with *some* idea of the constraints you may place on the exposition of the topic, and the second will provide you with pertinent knowledge that will help you and the teacher agree on how the finished Review will be constructed.

Don't be dismayed if the first of these discussions is less than totally productive from your point of view – the teacher may wish you to have a thoroughly wide scope in acquiring and handling information, and so may be extremely reticent about setting what look like 'limits' on your learning activity. Just accept this, and bear in mind that Literature Reviews are a recognised academic product; as such, certain ground rules apply about what they are and what they are not. Your teacher knows this. When you return for the second discussion, demonstrating your efforts to date, the potential boundaries of your Review will be much more obvious to you both, and you will have a solid basis on which to negotiate the *practical* scope of the finished piece.

If you haven't read the chapters in this book dealing with the use of textbooks, journals and the preparation of essays, do so now. The mechanics of collecting information *are* addressed here, but the picture will be rounded out with how information will be handled in the Review, and you may want a simpler starting point.

INFORMATION COLLECTING

You know already that information is available to you from three sources:

1. People
2. Printed text
3. Electronic text

and you can add an important fourth source: you. Reviews require more than the production of a synopsis of various data. They are thematic works of precision writing, where the author stays faithful to source material while exploring the meaning that it may have. However, since this author is acting as a channel for other peoples' work and ideas, it is important to consider how that channel may function. In other words, how will you behave as the author of a Literature Review? Will the information you acquire be allowed free and unrestricted access to your Review, will it be subtly altered in some way, added to or deleted from, or perhaps even be denied access? The point is, of course, that for every piece of information flowing through your mediumship as the Review's author, *another* piece emerges in the finished work. *Every* scrap of data that finds its way onto the pages of the Review will have been handled by you in some way; it will have been exposed to your thinking, your perceptions, values, belief systems, attitudes, opinions, likes and dislikes. Will it emerge unscathed as a 'true' representation of the original? Or will it be warped in some minor or major detail?

Stepping into the realm of reviewing and reporting other people's work demands certain things from you, certain outlooks, skills and behaviour that will serve the academic ends of the exercise.

First, you must be totally aware, at all times, of how your own knowledge and personal attributes may influence the contents of the Review. And you must seek to offset any individual characteristics of your own that might disorder or deny information that doesn't 'fit' your own viewpoint.

In short, you must be objective in acquiring and handling information. This includes the intention to observe yourself and evaluate how your personal stock of knowledge and store of information interacts with new information. That sounds cold and difficult, I know, but there's no substitute for it. Assessing 'outside' information is necessary – assessing your reaction to it is vital. This self-assessment must be continuous in writing a Review.

Second, you must be at pains never to misrepresent another author's work, either in substance by careless transcription, or in intention by careless interpretation. In other words, you must make every effort to ensure that any reporting of any author's message is as true to the original as you can possibly make it.

It doesn't matter how strongly you feel, either way, about the author's work. It's his or her product and you can't tamper with it. You have every right to say you think it's a load of nonsense, or that it's the best thing since sliced bread, but you do not have the right to change it.

You should note especially here that misrepresentation needn't have a 'malicious' or 'beneficial' origin. The unconsidered quoting of material *in the wrong context* can be enough to change the meaning of some information. You have to protect the integrity of other people's work, and guard against a thoughtless presentation of their message.

Third, the support or dismissal of material in a Review must be backed up in an acceptable way. You must proffer a foundation to any opinion that you choose to express, and not just where you say that some piece of information is 'right' or 'wrong'. If you have chosen, for any reason, to omit material from the Review that might have been included in other circumstances or by another author, then you should identify that reason for the reader.

By doing this, you're declaring your stance on the 'missing' material, making your own perspective plain, and allowing the reader the opportunity to evaluate your opinion.

It won't have escaped your notice that these last few passages have come close to describing everybody's picture of the cool, detached, sensible, careful academic perspective: and that's right. You're in this business now and are required to think and act in particular ways when it comes to obtaining, using and explaining information. 'Doing' a Literature Review is not just *practice* for academic behaviour – it *is* academic behaviour. Adopting the appropriate outlook and being mindful to stay within the groundrules is required of you *now*.

It's true to say that the activity it takes to complete your first Review will have you juggling research material while climbing a learning curve, and the effort required can be substantial; but it's worth it. Taking your place in a profession demands that you should possess the attribute of being able to initiate and direct your own continuing education. Mastering the skills and abilities that are needed to produce a good Literature Review will see you a long way down the road you have to travel.

With your topic established, and in the right frame of mind, you're ready to begin searching for the information you need. I recommend that you make a start on this as soon as you can. Don't put it off, start creating a knowledge base for yourself about the topic immediately. Where Reviews are concerned, it's never too soon to start identifying and collecting material.

Most people doing a Review head straight for the electronic help of CD ROMs and literature compilations such as CINAHL and MEDLINE, and these will prove of great use to you, too; but first, you have to ask yourself how much about the topic do you already know? Is it enough to let you select relevant items for further study from what might be a vast field of published information? The ocean of computerised data is one thing, the net you will fashion in order to fish around in it is quite another. Leave the hardware alone for a while, and start talking to people. Select *them* with care and, by the time you sit down at the computer, you'll be in a much fitter condition to start fishing.

Somewhere in a place you can reach personally, is a human being who knows something about the topic of your Review. And *elsewhere*, at the end of a telephone line and with a regular mail service to the door, are other human beings who might be experts in the subject of the topic. Most of them, if not every last one of them, will be pleased to hear from a learner who contacts them and makes a courteous request for educational help and advice.

How do you find them, and what do you say when you track them down?

1. Discuss your intentions with the staff of the institution in which your course is being held. They are much more in touch with what's happening than you are. Get the names and addresses of people who can help you from them, and don't forget to assure them sincerely that you will be polite and considerate to everybody concerned if you contact them as a learner associated with the present institution. Write a 'contact letter' for your teachers to cast an eye over before you send anything out in writing. Remember your manners. If you come up with a few good names, go on to point 4 below. If not, read on.

2. Write to the teaching staff of every educational institution in your city which deals with the subject of your Review, explaining what you want concisely and precisely. If you're given a contact, say Thank You and follow it up as recommended below. If not, read on.

3. Scan the Journals for *recent* publications on your topic subject, and write a letter to the author(s) outlining your request for information. Very few journals publish author's full addresses, so you may have to package your letter in another envelope containing a covering letter to the journal editor, asking that your original letter be addressed and forwarded to the author. Most journals are prepared to do this, so give it a go if you need to.

   You might also consider having a request for information published in a journal's letter column, where you make it clear that you're interested in *discussing* your topic subject with knowledgeable individuals. Responses to these letters can be patchy, though, and time-consuming. But it's certainly worth a try.

4. Once you have a list of people who can (at least putatively) help you out, get in touch with them. Don't be hesitant. The worst they can do is to ignore you. Telephone calls are best for establishing contact and making appointments to see someone. *Don't* turn up unannounced.

   If the idea of phoning a stranger and asking for information leaves you squirming, or if the individual is sufficiently far away to make a call economically hazardous, sit down and write a very nice letter with the details of your request prefaced by an acknowledgement of their expertise in the subject field and an expression of gratitude for the help and advice you **hope** they will deliver.

Sitting down face to face with your 'expert' is best, but if it can't be arranged, don't worry about it, and don't go to extraordinary lengths to achieve it. An exchange of letters can be more than adequate. Remember, when you're asking someone to write back, to enclose a stamped, addressed envelope for them to use. It costs very little, but it might assure you of a response, besides being polite.

5. Here's your contact then, sitting across from you, at the end of a phone, or picking up a pen to write back. What enquiry do you make of them? It comes in two parts – Perspective and Direction.

Perspective

You want to know how the expert views the field of information, what they see as fundamental to an understanding of the topic. A list of prepared questions along these lines will help:

- What issues are currently to the fore in the field?
- Do these issues have equally 'important' contributions to make in extending the knowledge and understanding of the subject?
- Or does one of them appear to be especially significant in some way?
- What 'seminal' works in the field can be identified?
- In any Literature Review of the field, what material could be identified as being *essential* for inclusion?

Direction

You want to know how the expert evaluates information on the subject, how they approach the body of knowledge in terms of discriminating between the 'worth' of one contribution and another:

- What *kind* of material contributes most to developing a knowledge and understanding of the subject?
- Does any particular type of approach which seeks to explore and explain the topic seem inappropriate or unhelpful?

In this way, perspective lets you grasp a potted version of how someone knowledgeable in the field views the topic, and direction helps point you towards an understanding of the values they hold that influence that view. The point is that while you want to acquire a useful preliminary knowledge base so that your approach to the beginning of your Review will be reasonably informed, your best starting point is to be prepared to scrutinise everything you learn in terms of how it is affected by the person who handles it. We've already discussed the most important human agency in this – you – and it's just as important for you to remember that any information that comes your way has been produced by another fallible individual. In other words, your 'expert' may be learned, but they are not the Oracle. They may be extremely clever and a shining light in the field, but they are not without humdrum values, such as a reluctance to acknowledge their own prejudices.

We're covering the possibilities of 'wayward' influences on the handling of information here in terms of your personal contact with people, but the same holds true when you start delving into the literature. Behind every glossy feature article, terse critique or fact-packed research report is a human being. Whether you will eventually accept their message or reject it is not the sole issue, but many of us behave as though it were, and our use of critical thinking, of analysis and evaluation, is given an energy input that ensures we arrive at one of just two decisions about information – 'This is right' or 'This is wrong'.

There is no better time than *now* for you as a learner to equip yourself with an attitude that will always bring critical thinking into play when you are faced with information and 'asked' to incorporate it into your knowledge base. Start as you mean to go on, in the full recognition that no information, from whatever quarter it may originate, will escape your balanced scrutiny, and in the full acceptance that this kind of outlook generates activity that requires effort. To do otherwise is to go through your learning experiences in the belief that swallowing received opinion is a perfectly adequate substitute for learning. It isn't, but it's plagued the profession for a long, long time.

I'm going on about this at length because I want you to enjoy putting your Review together. A task like this can be time-consuming and appear onerous – if you see it just as a course requirement. Of course it is, but that doesn't mean it has to be dealt with in a mechanistic let's-get-it-over-with way. The best thing you can bring to the Review is an active and inquisitive mind, one that's prepared to stay fresh and awake and aware of how learning takes place. Your teachers can do certain things to help you learn, but the course will end at some point; the shape of the mind you take into the profession is up to you.

Having considered what your experts had to tell you you've made a start on constructing a knowledge base, and you may well already have started to develop a degree of insight into the material. Your next step is to begin investigating the body of literature available – the heart of which will be found in the library. Which library? The biggest and best to which you have unrestricted access, encompassing all the facilities you need for your research, or otherwise able to secure information for you which is not currently on disk, paper or sitting as texts on shelves.

With a brief summary to hand of what you already know about the topic, put yourself first in the middle of the *electronic* web of information. Chase every data compilation disk that notes details of publications which you might, even tangentially, find informative. Quiz every last one of them as fully as you can, and don't worry about accumulating a mountain of references which you will ultimately have to sift through to get at the nuggets of gold buried within. Set very few limits on your computerised searches for information; you're reaching out for every-thing that's there, and you don't yet know enough to tell the gold from the dross.

You may find that the instruction you receive on your course about the use of CD-ROM software guides you towards preparing very specific 'questions' with which to interrogate a data base. That's fine; very sens-ibly based on the premise that you don't have forever to sit in front of a PC. However, with a bit of thought, you can see that a wide-based enquiry can still focus on single points – points which can be ordered in relation to their importance to you. So, while you might construct specific questions, their *range* must be sufficiently wide to allow you a freedom of access to possibly pertinent material.

Never inhibit a literature search by a 'rule' which you have not thought through with care, especially if it might serve to close off avenues of enquiry which you believe should be at least considered.

Let's take an example or two of how you might frame data base 'questions', starting with the topic title given earlier:

'The practical application of nursing audit'

The first thing to do is to refine into headings what you believe to be the *operative* issues in your Review. That is; try to define the most basic concepts contained in the topic, those which are fundamental to the material, and translate these into *named areas* for enquiry. A short set of 'questions' might look like this:

1. 'Nursing Audit'
2. 'Audit in Nursing Practice'
3. 'Clinical Audit in Nursing'
4. 'Quality Assurance in Nursing Practice'
5. 'Application of Quality Assurance in Clinical Care'
6. 'Principles and Practice of Nursing Audit'

Plus, of course, the inclusion of the topic title itself – if it's short and salient. Achieving any access to an arm of the relevant material on disk will supply you with reams of further 'question' structures as you come to recognise the terminology and appreciate how the pertinent publications can be made available. When the first reference set scrolls down the screen, pay it very close attention indeed – **don't** be tempted to skimp on identifying material you want collated and printed. Finer selectivity can come later, just get your hands on the first set and read it very carefully.

You're not done with the PC yet, but leave it for now and start tracking down the most promising items in your first reference set. It can be very tempting to sit before the screen and dream up 'question' after 'question' in an attempt to do all the spadework at once. Resist it. Coming to grips with the literature means getting your hands on printed pages.

Get your notebook out, buy a card for the nearest photocopier, and head straight for the shelves where, from your reference list, you're looking first for:

Literature Reviews

If any recent reviews have been published on your topic, pick these up and be thankful. Read and reread them with a searching and critical eye. Make copious notes. Compare your reference list with that given for the review(s) and expand your list with any new material presented. Soak it all up and consider it very carefully. Take as much time as you need to learn what it has to teach you, not only in terms of 'hard' information, but of how that information is handled and written about.

Don't be dismayed that someone else has 'beaten you to it'. You're a learner learning and besides, remember that no two people will view the same information in exactly the same way; not only do you have every right to compile your own Review, but a fresh set of perceptions deployed on *any* material can have beneficial results. It is *not* beyond the bounds of possibility that the next review to be published on the topic will have your name on it.

Now that you're among the literature, a cautionary note must be raised about the nature of the information you will read about, learn from and perhaps use.

Original Sources

With the necessary burden on you to present someone else's work clearly and without bias or alteration in an academic piece, the first requirement is obvious – you should have read for yourself what that person had to say. This sounds perfectly straightforward, but circumstances can conspire to lead you away from a consideration and reporting of these original sources of information. The author's work might be difficult to obtain, perhaps even long out of print, or tucked away in some forgotten nook of only the very biggest Reference Libraries. In cases like these, by far the easiest course to take in discussing the material at all is to report on what a second author had to say about the first. Of course, the second author too might not have been able to acquire an original material source either, so that the report they wrote might have been based on a digest prepared by a third author, whose own work may or may not have been produced from a contact with the original. It's getting more complicated now – more people are inserting themselves between the source and you, every one of whom might have 'influenced' the information in an important way and introduced potential biases into the understanding of the information which you will not be able to recognise.

The best and brightest analytical thinking can go for nothing if the basic material is flawed by misrepresentation.

The only truly acceptable stance for reviewing another person's work is for you to be intimately acquainted with the original material. However, as a learner with limited time and resources at your disposal, some original sources might prove to lie beyond your capacity to acquire them. There's not a great deal you can do about that, but you *must* recognise that any second-hand or third-hand or tenth-hand versions of the original are exactly that – *versions*: they must be reported as such by you. For example:

If you have an original source to hand, quote it and then draw infer-ences from it and make comments; the reader can make up their own mind about what you have to say and can, because you've provided them with a reference for the material, read it for themselves and evaluate both the original material and yours. If you are working from someone else's version of a piece of information and you state this clearly, giving a reference that indicates the two sources of the material, the reader is made aware that your handling of the information is derived from a secondary source, and may choose to 'step up' their analytical scrutiny of what you have to say.

So, while you should work from original source material wherever possible, you must take special care in handling and reporting informa-tion drawn from secondary sources. The further away from the original your information is, the more the onus falls on you to treat it with caution and to present it as fairly and as truthfully as you can.

Some people don't, and we might as well stare this aspect of human nature straight in the face and get it out of the way. Some people, in using the work of other authors, find it irresistibly convenient to present it as their own, thereby saving themselves much effort. This activity is known as plagiarism, and no field of published academic literature is entirely free from it. You might, at dark moments in your education, come to believe that *any* and *all* academic literature is virtually no more than a succession of new publications rehashing old knowledge. But this rehashing, where sometimes excruciatingly small differences in the handling of information prompt the covering of a lot of 'old' ground, is a very different matter from passing off someone else's work as your own. A piece of academic literature might be 95 per cent composed of previous work by other people, but so long as *all* of this work is properly acknowledged, the 5 per cent original contribution by the author is still valid, still acceptable. The rules of academic writing in handling another author's work go beyond the display of professional courtesy – they are meant to protect individual rights in retaining a clear ownership of 'intellectual property'. The Copyright Laws are the fiscal arm of this protection, meant to underscore the importance of the author's interests when his or her work is found in the public domain. It's just as important to recognise that while information is there to be acquired, adopted, adapted, handled and learned from, it cannot be reproduced in its original state as though it were being newly minted.

That said, we can go back to your Literature Review.

Whether or not you find previously published reviews, stay with the journals and seek next for:

Research Papers

if indeed there are any available in your subject. There may not be, but do your level best to find any that may exist. Track down any published material that handles some aspect of the topic in a critical, investigative way – in an experimental setting or as a survey report, or whatever. Good research papers demonstrate a *use* of knowledge and can provide you with much more than just an A–B–C route through the material. The results of research might or might not be particularly illuminating, but the declaration of the author's inferences and conclusions can assist you greatly in developing a sharper insight and understanding of how relevant information can be approached and handled.

If you do acquire a number of research-based articles, examine the reference lists given for each and every one of them and, as before, compare it with your (amended) reference list and add to it where possible. You might think we're heading for overkill here on the accrual of reference sources, but it can be very instructive to see how different authors utilise different information bases with which to address the 'same' issue. So don't be too concerned if your reference list seems to acquire a life of its own. You will learn from it now, and then prune it later if necessary.

Now, a word about photocopying. If you've got time and money enough to make a photocopy of every relevant article of literature you find, I would be the last person to tell you to go easy on creating a paper mountain, for the very good reason that there is no substitute for having a personal copy of written material which you can peruse at leisure when-ever the occasion demands it. However, the other side of the coin is that it is very unlikely that you will either need (or could use) every scrap of information you acquire in a literature search. Some degree of selectivity has to be introduced so that you retain or discard material in a sensible way. If you're unsure about the validity of your selection process, which should of course be based on your understanding of the topic, make sure that you know exactly how to recover access to literature that you 'dismiss' on your first pass through the data. Take the time to add a few details on each item contained in your reference list, describing *where* it can be found, *what* it contained and *why* you decided not to use it.

The least you should do with every piece of research material you find is to make an accurate note of the contents of the Abstract: word-for-word is best, so that if you trawl through your 'discarded' references later, you can be assured that the information upon which you can base a decision to dig something out again is accurate.

In possession of your Reviews (if any) and research-based material (hopefully), you can start casting wider for less specific, but no less germane, literature:

Critiques, Commentaries, Feature Articles

First, I'll put a qualifier on the inclusion of 'critiques' here – it is possible to find specific, single-pointed critiques aimed at one aspect of one author's work, and these can be very helpful indeed. However, you might more often run across critiques where broad information bases are used as a vehicle for the major theme of the article, and your use of them has to be governed with regard to how specific they are in fact when dealing with your topic. Here, as with any material you might use, the original *context* in which the material is presented has to be evaluated with care. It's sometimes all too easy in reading critiques to construe a general remark by the author to be solely and specifically linked with your subject of interest. Dipping into a critique for a single 'good' or 'bad' item can put you in the middle of a minefield.

However, I would recommend that you seek out these three types of literature in the order given above. Note particularly how any examples of each handle the information they draw on for their contents. Remember to compare references again and amend your list if required, and bear in mind that 'feature' articles might not be academically rigorous, but they can be informative.

Last, you can move to the material you'll probably use first in your Review –

Textbooks and Publications by 'Official Bodies'

If the topic you're reviewing is represented in textbooks then these will of course inform and underwrite your knowledge base. You should chase them down and use them – mostly for your learning. You're preparing a Literature Review, not a Book Review, delivering a wide perspective on a field of knowledge, not a discourse on how the instruction on a subject is written about.

Aim to get your hands on authoritative texts that are recognised as being essential reading on the topic, preferably ones that are written by an author still active in the field. If you get access to an example of a textbook that is perenially popular, and regularly revised and updated, use the most recent edition. As always, check your reference list against any noted in the book.

'Occasional Papers', 'Reports', 'Policy Statements (or Analyses)', 'Guidelines' and other publications by statutory and/or voluntary agencies might be available which deal 'officially' with some aspect of your topic. Don't be tempted to pass these by: some of them might put you off by the encyclopaedic detail they contain – 99.9 per cent of which you have no current use for; others might be written in a special form of opaque and tiring jargon. Never mind, press on. Give them attention if they can be of any possible use to you – they might be the most accurate sources of information you can lay your hands on. Don't forget to look for references.

Now all you have to do is to assimilate the information you've gathered together, consider it at length, re-search your research, and then write your Review. The more time and effort you put into the first two of these will make the third easier and the fourth straightforward.

ASSIMILATION AND CONSIDERATION

The best way to start is to order your material so that you read from a 'basic and general' level of information and move through various stages of acquiring 'progressive and specific' knowledge of the topic, making notes as you go. More of this in a moment.

Your initial 'reading order' might look like this -

1. *Textbook 'primer'*:   (plainly describing fundamental issues and explaining the subject with the intention to instruct)
2. *'Reference' textbook*:   (comprehensive and fully detailed text aiming to provide an 'expert' grasp of the subject)
3. *'Research papers'*
4. *Critiques*
5. *Commentaries*
6. *Publications by statutory and voluntary agencies*
7. *'Feature' articles*

You can see that the phrase 'progressive and specific' refers to the accumulation process rather than to any inherent qualities of the material.

Settling down to read your way through what might be a daunting stack of papers, books and reports in preparation for writing a Literature Review can sometimes serve to induce an attack of the 'anti-academic' vapours, characterised by a devout wish to be elsewhere and the desire to take up an easier, less exacting occupation. If this happens to you, just ignore it. Pick up the first item on your reading list and make a start.

Take it slowly enough so that you *handle* the material from the word go – don't just scan, skip or sprint your way along some erratic and formless 'path', skirting thick tomes and ignoring the small print. A well-organised beginning will prevent your collected data from turning rapidly into a haphazard jumble of semi-digested disconnected bits and pieces. From the very outset, you should be determined to assimilate information, consider it with care and make notes on everything you read, and most of what you think when you read it. A few guidelines on this will help.

REVIEW THINKING AND REVIEW NOTES

Push yourself into thinking about everything you read, and acquire the habit of looking for relationships between one piece of published data and another, where these relationships are significant in some way and provide (or possibly provide) an avenue whereby the information may be better explained, explored, highlighted, understood, supported, undermined – and a host of other qualifiers and descriptors. From square one, as your stock of knowledge accumulates, try to view each piece of data as both an item in itself and as a piece of a larger 'whole'. This last 'holistic' view has as much to do with the nature of your Review as it has to do with the subject itself, and is dependent upon your growing grasp of the topic – so don't worry if the early stages of your preparation leave you little the wiser. As time passes, you'll find that as your overall appreciation of the topic becomes deeper and more detailed, the number of authors' viewpoints represented in the literature helps you secure a usefully 'sophisticated' perspective on the information. This 'maturing' of your outlook on the material will serve you very well, but it can only be acquired by doing the things necessary to attain it, by making the effort to create a detailed and relevant knowledge base.

As you read . . . think. As you think . . . make notes – which should go beyond headings and cryptic remarks. From the moment you first pick up your pen, be sure that your note-taking will be extensive and thorough. You're trying to distil a sensible piece of connected and logical written work out of reams of data, and there's no time like the present to start reducing it to familiar 'handled' material placed in the context of your own thoughts.

The guidelines for review note-taking will help you do that

(a) Use a separate sheet (or sheets) of A4 paper to make notes on every source of information you use. At the top, write out a full reference for the piece. If it's a research article with an Abstract, or some other summary is given, note this in detail. Now rule off two vertical lines splitting the page into three columns. Head these columns as shown in the Figure.

THIS SOURCE	OTHER SOURCES	COMMENTS

(b) As you read the piece, use the first column to make notes on salient items and pertinent issues – facts, figures, the chronology of events, special emphases made by the author, comments, conclusions, references to other work in the field, essential or otherwise notable elements about the subject, the constraints and opportunities on implementing research activity, perceptions expressed on the consensus or disagreement of opinion about any matter, authors' recommendations for further study and investigation, departures from 'accepted' thinking on the subject, innovations, policy decisions as 'rules' in the public domain . . . These, and any other data that strike you as pertinent, will feed your understanding of the material and should be paid close attention.

(c) As the first column fills, think 'around' the subject of each entry and note particular thoughts in the 'Comments' column. Don't worry if your first pass through the data leaves this column depressingly blank, you'll be coming back to it as your knowledge base grows.

(d) When you've thoroughly gone over every scrap of data in your possession, take your notes for each piece of literature and compare the contents of every first column with the others. Take your time, make your scrutiny searching enough to discover any possible correspondences between what different authors have written: connections, relationships, agreement, disagreement, 'verification', supportive statements or dismissive opinions, mutually held or contradictory 'truths' about 'facts' . . . any and all putative links should be identified and recorded in the 'Other Sources' columns, prefaced by a *brief* description of the type of correspondence displayed, for example, '*Agreement*' or '*Supported by*'. Be careful with these entries – transcribe information carefully from your first columns over into 'Other Sources' columns in sufficient detail to illuminate the nature of the link.

Now, it's worth stating the obvious. You might be reluctant to check every page of your notes against every other page. Don't be tempted to discard each page of notes as it's compared with the others. Keep it in the pile, and rotate it through the process of comparison as many times as it is required. Checking and rechecking data is part and parcel of ensuring that accuracy is maintained and your learning is supported. Data duplications between the first and second columns of various pages might be numerous, which is perfectly acceptable at this stage. If your comparison of data is thorough, the 'Other Sources' columns will be replete with material 'cross-referenced' to the items appearing in the first column, and duplication allows you increased opportunities to check up on the acuity of your research for correspondences. Your work on these notes is very unlikely to be done at a single sitting, and you might be surprised to discover how your viewpoint on data changes as your learning and understanding increase in breadth and depth.

(e) When the contents of the first and second columns are as complete and as detailed as you can make them, they will contain between them most of the material that you will need for your Review – either as 'stand-alone' singular items or as clusters of 'related' data. Now is the time to go through all of it again and make notes in your 'Comments' column.

Take each entry in the first column and consider it at length, either in a general perspective on the entire subject if you have found no links with other materal in your collected literature, or in tandem with any cross-referenced material. What is important about this data, what should you know and understand about it? What does it have to contribute to an holistic view of the topic?

Be at pains to stay as objective as you can when you make these comments, and keep them brief, very much to the point, and free from any Value Added Tosh. There's room in your final Review to make a personal statement or two, but it's best to keep your notes cool and detached for the present. When your notes are complete, take each item dealt with across the three columns and check it against the original sources of information and ask yourself these questions:

- Is every scrap of data which has been transcribed in its original form accurately reproduced?
- Does every rewording, rephrasing or 'translation' still remain faithful to the original meaning and convey the same message?
- Are the correspondences you've identified between pieces of information still evident to you when the sets of original sources are compared again?

Be ruthless with yourself and your notes when you do this exercise. Accuracy is the overwhelming principle here and must be served to the point of exhaustion. It will all pay off in a good Review.

(f) Now, with all your information identified, referenced, cross-referenced, thought about, checked, verified and thought about again, it's time to start knocking it into shape. Which begins with thinking about it some more.

FRAMEWORK AND CONTEXT

What shape should your Review take, how will it begin, middle along and then end? Will it be a streamlined piece of precision writing or a syntactical jungle where a forest of facts is hung about with stringy remarks? Will you use grandiose prose like this, or be sensibly contented with plain speaking?

Writing Literature Reviews has a tendency to frighten people, since they are, so far as learners are concerned, specially prepared exhibits of the level of effort and intellectual ability of which the individual is capable. Fair enough, I can't deny that, and you probably can't stop thinking about it; but don't stare it in the face long enough to be mesmerised by fear and what-ifs. There are too many benefits to be gained from researching and writing Reviews to permit just one (current) aspect of the business to prejudice your outlook and perhaps even have a negative effect on the final results of your work. By this stage you've already done the hard bit, so ignore the total size of the task if it bothers you. You're already more than half-way to completion of your Review, and it's going to be worth every minute of the time and energy it took you to do.

First, as I've said already, stick closely to any guidelines you're given which make any particular demands of the finished piece, especially with regard to the imposition of rules about the order in which the contents are presented and the system of textual references. I'll cover these and other points in some detail below but remember that your final work has to satisfy your assessors, not me.

Framework

A simple way to organise your Review is to present it in the following order:

Beginning	Abstract
	Introduction
Middle	Presentation of data
	Exposition of topic
End	Discussion
	Reference List

Abstract

An abstract is a brief digest of what the Review has to say. It should be short, salient, accurate and very much to the point, conveying the main message(s) of the text with as much clarity as you can muster. Don't write your abstract until you've produced a final draft of the Review, which should be pored over with fanatical care before the abstract is constructed – make very, very sure your abstract reflects the contents of the Review, strictly that and no more.

Don't fret if it takes you four or 44 attempts to produce a good abstract. There's an art and a science to it which take time and practice to acquire.

Introduction

Your introduction should quickly acquaint the reader with two things – *what* you're going to be talking about and *why* you're talking about it at all. As concisely as possible, identify and explain the topic and give reasons for its selection as the subject of a Review.

The 'naming and describing' of the Topic may seem a little superfluous to you, because you're immersed in the material, but take nothing for granted on behalf of the reader – make short, plain statements about the topic.

The reasons you give for the topic's presentation in a Review should be drawn from some phenomenon of interest about the subject covered. A few examples of these are given below:

- a complete absence of Literature Reviews produced in the field;
- no recent reviews published in an expanding field;
- a rapidly developing field where an abundance of literature is regularly published from a number of sources; and
- an innovation, sudden advance in knowledge or new perspective, which serves to permit or encourage a different understanding of material in the field.

Essentially, your Introduction sets the scene for what is to follow, giving the reader a handle on the Review. This is the place to make broad summary statements about the topic, and precise information from instructive textbooks can provide you with exactly the right kind of 'hooks' you need upon which to hang the rest of your explanation, followed perhaps, if the subject allows it, by some supportive or contradictory material culled from recent research.

Spend time on your Introduction so that it reads well and says what you want it to say, but don't let it get away from you and become too lengthy. It serves as 'opener' to the rest of your Review.

Presentation of data

This should be as clear, concise and precise as you can possibly make it. We'll be covering how to order the sequence of your material in the section that follows this one, but it's vital that you concentrate first on ensuring maximum accuracy, for both individual items of data and the way in which two or more items are presented together in a putative relationship.

In the presentation of a single piece of information drawn from another author's work, you know that the rigid application of referencing rules should prevent any confusion in the reader's mind about the source of the data. This issue is covered in detail in Chapter 4; but for your Review writing, you can see that with a welter of 'external' source material to accommodate, the application of the referencing rules can be a tricky business. Information from one source might sit cheek-by-jowl with highly similar information from a different source; almost entire paragraphs might be jam-packed with items of data with double, triple or quadruple references, no one of which 'agrees' with any other. The onus is on you to ensure that all of it remains a faithful representation of the original material, stays germane to the topic, and never strays beyond the bounds of clarity.

This is a tall order, especially for the novice, but of course it can be done. It just takes – you know I'm going to say *time* and *practice*. If your first efforts at constructing this 'body' of your Review ends up in a total mess – be patient with yourself and the material. Doing this presentation of data well requires skill; give yourself a chance to acquire it. A few hints and words of caution might help, contained in two sections, each dealing with the principle influences on the handling of the Review data – You and Other Authors.

YOU

You are the most important 'internal' influence on how information will be dealt with in the Review, so look to yourself first as the crucial author represented in the piece. Other people's data has to fit with yours, so write as well as you can. Don't let the nature of a Review seduce you into thinking you're just there to squeeze the 'glue' words between slices of information – *'and'*, *'but'*, *'whereas'*, *'recently'*, *'before'*, *'although'*. Set out with the intention to communicate clearly and make every word of your own count as an essential contribution to the sense of the overall piece.

Never bother your head with notions of semantic perfection for the sake of beautifying prose. The best Reviews are like houses built out of those little plastic bricks: the final shape is unmistakeable and a coherent whole, but you can also see every last little component, the differences between them and how they're joined together.

If you get stuck in the middle of what becomes a horrifyingly complicated data presentation, look first to your own efforts at putting it together and consider what you might have been thinking when you started – for example:

- Have you been scribbling down your notes word for word, with no thought for any discontinuity between them?
- Has the apparent authority of printed literature beguiled you into thinking you have no right to write yourself into the company of *real* authors?
- Has your native wit deserted you and been replaced by fear?

- Were the data collection and the writing of the Review separated by too long an interval? In other words, has the writing been shelved until memory and understanding have started to fade?

If the answer to any of these is 'yes', then the remedies are straightforward: attitude correction and more work sums them up fairly well. If the answer to all of them is 'no', then you can start to scrutinise the data itself for any possible problems in presentation, beginning with the blatantly obvious:

- Have you tried to say too much?

which is an easy thing to do: either for the whole Review, in which case the most likely problem is that you've overstepped the bounds of the 'phenomenon of interest' by a large margin and you need to rein yourself in and become much more specific about your inclusion of material; or for different parts of the Review, where the presentation of material might need to differ from 'sparse but telling' to 'discursive but instructive', but you've gone for broke and sprinted away in the pursuit of trivia and bulked out the material till the buttons popped. On the other hand:

- Have you said too little?

There is no place more arid in which to find yourself than the parchingly dry gullies between one dusty little piece of information and another, unconnected dusty little piece of information. Fertile ground for thoughtful writing it isn't. If you've selected your literature with care, creaking to a series of frustrating stops in writing about it might be due to the omission of too much of the subject. It's possible to narrow down the scope of your Review to the point where you'll squeeze all the juice out of the information you present. Stay pertinent, but widen it out a little until you can (this is very poetic) dip your pen into a free flow of information and write with ease. This solution also works with a problem similar to writing too little, where Review material is scanty but the relevant question is:

- Have you bent the data out of shape?

Good Reviews shrink a wealth of data into a manageable size, but where the focus of this reduction should be on isolating and identifying salient issues in a rigorous representation of original messages; it can be a deceptively simple matter to reduce data so much that they become small masses of unrecognisable pulp. That's a bit strong, but it happens. Warping information by condensing it with too much zeal and not enough regard for the depth and breadth of the message it contains can make a Review grind to a halt, and it can be very difficult to work out how to get it started again. The point is that if you could read what you'd written with no memory of how it got onto the page, you'd see fuzzy messages loosely associated with what appears to be baseless connections. Between reading and understanding your source material, making notes and then preparing the Review, your grasp of the subject might be very good indeed, to the extent that when you condense data, instead of coming out as a logical precis embodying all the sense and meaning of the original, information appears in your writing as a kind of idiosyncratic shorthand which might well trigger *your* understanding but will leave the reader totally adrift. You can recognise when this happens fairly easily – you start stumbling over what you thought would be straightforward bits of prose: a passage or a paragraph starts to crumble when you add another bit of information. It stops making sense, and when you reread it to discover what the problem is, you find it runs off in unusual directions, or you blank out completely on what it means until you bring the rest of what you know about it into play. The meaning it should have is lost, and no amount of grammatical fiddling will bring it back. The solution is to re-search the data source and inject your writing with the original messages, because what you've got on paper now is an over-filtered hodge-podge from which you've drained most of the vital ingredients.

The last thing I'll mention about you as the Review author is to remind you that you *are* an author. You are intent on composing an original piece of written work; what else could you be but an author? So, treat yourself with some respect and remember that you and your writing have a rightful place to occupy among other authors.

OTHER AUTHORS

First, some heresy: a fair proportion of published professional authors can't write. They're knowledgeable, and might be well-educated, well-read, highly qualified, experienced and smart as a whip; but when it comes to constructing lucid prose and communicating in print, they're non-starters. Why are they published then, you may ask? The answer is that what they attempt to write about is probably well worth knowing, that's why. They break into print because while their writing might lack clarity and be difficult to read, their ideas have value and their work is significant.

So, if referenced data which you wish to include in your Review is salient, but difficult to understand because of the way in which it was written about by the original author, the way in which *you* transpose the material into the Review is of vital importance. For example:

Using direct quotes

If you're using a straight quote, is there anything about it which serves to obscure the message or require explanation? We're getting dangerously close to making subjective judgments here rather than objective evaluations, but the matter has to be considered. Quoting an author's own words can be a useful way to encapsulate messages, and might be the most accurate way to do so. However, you can't swamp your Review with streams of quotes; you have to go beyond demonstrating a knowledge of something and move into the higher cognitive reaches of your brainpower and display an ability to handle information via analysis and so on. Besides, and more to the point for our purposes here, we can quietly bear in mind that an author's message is not always most clearly conveyed in the words he or she has chosen to use. Direct quotes have to be chosen and transposed with *extreme* care – they must be pertinent, highly specific and placed in an unarguably *relevant* context. All right, a well-chosen quote which is clearly written and situated correctly in your Review in an appropriate context is an excellent way of representing the original author's point of view. I'm not saying don't use them, but use them sparingly and at need and keep them brief. And, if you find that quoting directly from an original source turns out to be problematic, consider the following:

1. Is there anything about the quoted material that *does* seem to obscure the message and require explanation? Perhaps the injudicious use of jargon or a less than felicitous use of ordinary language? Are sentences tortuously long, containing a single salient datum plastered over with distracting trivia?
2. Are references made within the quote, either obliquely or directly, to information which either the Review does not contain elsewhere, or which the reader might not know?

The major points with which to illuminate the solutions to dealing with 'difficult' quotes are straightforward, and revolve around your understanding whether the inclusion of a quote does in fact transmit a message informatively and with accuracy. If, in your best and most considered evaluation of the issue covered, you suspect that the quote fails to meet either of these two criteria, then don't quote. Move to the second method of conveying other author's messages:

Paraphrasing

in which information is restated with an especial concern for clarifying the message.

Paraphrasing is one of those indispensable and hugely valuable intellectual skills which is so closely ravelled up with learning, education and communication that we can stare it in the face every day of our lives and still fail to realise its true significance. A very great deal of what we learn will never be reproduced by us in any form *but* a paraphrasing of the original. This prompts us to pay very close attention to how we apply and develop this skill.

When it comes to preparing a Review, you must be sure that your paraphrasing is exact and appropriate. A few guidelines will help.

1. If original material contains 'x' number of points of information which go together to make a related whole, re-present them all. Don't lose vital data in order to condense information, or you may adversely affect the message. Be very careful about the *order* in which related points are given in the original; it may be highly pertinent.
2. Don't be tempted to 'clarify' messages by introducing jargon that replaces several 'ordinary' words with one polysyllabic monster.
3. Always check your paraphrasing against the original to make sure it delivers a faithful version of the information contained.
4. If you find that several attempts at paraphrasing still result in little more than a slightly rejigged copy of the original, using most of the first author's words and phrases, it might be that you don't fully understand the message and could usefully spend more time becoming acquainted with it before trying to rewrite it.
5. Be very careful about paraphrasing a single message and then referencing it by indicating other sources that agree or disagree with the issue represented, especially where these subsequent sources are themselves paraphrased. You can see that special care must be taken here – you've done a fair amount of data *handling* before you've come to data *presentation*. Make certain the foundation to all of it is rock-solid and accurate.
6. Don't worry if a good paraphrased example of a 'difficult' message is two or three times as long as the original. It if conveys a clear explana-

tion of the data and allows the information to be represented *in toto*, be content. You can always try to condense it a little, but don't fiddle with it for ever; your priority is to make the message understandable.

Finally, remember that while the presentation of data in your Review is in your hands, the majority of that data is 'owned' by someone else. They have a right to expect you to handle it with care: analysis, evaluation and the synthesis of information is grist to the mill of your learning and the writing of the Review – which is not the place for *correction* of other authors' work.

Exposition of topic

A well-ordered presentation of data goes a very long way to ensure a high quality Review, and the way in which you literally underwrite that quality is to deal sensibly with two equally important issues – Language and the Juxtaposition of information.

Language   The language you use for your Review should be plain and simple, knitted together in lucid prose that delivers information without delivering judgment at the same time.

You will have learned already that an appropriate 'academic' writing style is generally favoured, which strives for accuracy and objectivity in handling information. This style is drawn from the viewpoint that nothing is ever and always 'true' and even if something is, it is extremely unlikely that every one of us would ascribe the same value to it in every set of circumstances that could possibly arise. That's a clumsy way of saying that academic writers strive to 'lay out' information upon which the reader, perfectly prepared to analyse and evaluate the information personally, neither needs nor requires the superimposition of a value system which might in any way serve to hinder the balanced scrutiny of the material.

This type of writing can make stringent demands upon you, but a Review is an excellent forum for learning how to go about acquiring the habits of writing with a scrupulous regard for conveying information accurately and well. It's not too difficult to learn the basic 'rules' – it's their application in practice that can prove a trifle troublesome, if you don't grasp the necessity for adhering to them, that is. Essentially, though, where your Review is concerned, you don't have any room to manoeuvre, you must make the expected commitment to safeguarding 'truth' and supporting the reader's right to expect an even-handed presentation of the material. In doing so, you can consider the basic 'rules' as affecting both key individual words and phrases. For example, definitive words which assign permanent properties to material can be very easy to misuse and are rarely justified – *always* and *never* are two of these:

> 'Until 1957, the post of Hospital Matron was always filled by women in Britain, and never by a man.'

In writing a statement like this, you might be totally convinced that you're right, because you've either (a) swallowed somebody else's data without digestion or (b) exhaustively researched as much literature as you can get your hands on which deals with posts termed *Matron* where these were exclusively filled by women. But the awake and aware reader might wonder about 'hidden', perhaps influential data available from other sources which records the employment of a total of 28 men fulfilling similar roles in British hospitals whose job title was tailored for them to avoid the embarrassment of being called 'Matron'. Ah, you might say, but I'm using this information in context, and the next sentence will make everything clear. Well, why not make *this* sentence clear, since it too is part of the fabric of context? Especially if the next sentence also makes a definitive statement, one which relies on previous information to be understood? Such as:

> 'However, in September of 1957, Charles Brown SRN was appointed to the Board of St Kilda's General Hospital in Oxford, an event which some authors claim heralded a revolution in British nursing.'

It all begins to come apart at the seams, and a careful reader will begin to wonder more about both the accuracy of your data presentation and your handling of the material. The 'always' and 'never' descriptors have started the dissolution of your objective writing style, and served to colour the reception of your next statements.

Other examples of these descriptive words abound, and serve to 'qualify' data by the imposition of some value. For example:

> *Undoubtedly*, as in: 'The turgid style in which many Conceptual Models of Nursing are first described is *undoubtedly* a major factor influencing their sparse application in practice.'

whereas the reader has every right to doubt that this is the case, especially if they don't agree with your sarcastic remark about 'turgid' writing styles.

Obviously, as in: Some studies have shown that only 10 per cent of practising nurses can name and describe a Conceptual Model of Nursing Care, while other studies have found that 90 per cent of nursing practice is designed and delivered without any reference to a Conceptual Model. *Obviously,* the two findings are connected.'

where the only thing that's really 'obvious' is that you've jumped to a conclusion which, on the face of the 'evidence' presented, is completely unwarranted. There may or may not be a connection, and unless you're prepared to investigate the possibility in appropriate research activity, you certainly can't state that there is one.

Unarguably, as in: 'The consensus of opinion in the literature about the use of Conceptual Models of Nursing is that they are a waste of time. This is *unarguably* the case.'

It's nothing of the kind. A supporter of Conceptual Models might or might not find it easy to refute the first statement you've made, but they would have absolutely no difficulty in arguing about it.

You can see that with the adoption of a certain perspective on *all* information, most especially the bits you supply yourself, certain words and ways of phrasing things militate against a 'neutral' exposition of data.

Allied to the avoidance of value-laden terms is the 'rule' that carefully balanced 'value-free' words and phrases introduce the right note of detachment and objectivity into academic writing. For example:

Instead of: 'The way in which this study was put together is so obviously slap-dash that absolutely no reliance can be placed on the results.'

This becomes: 'It might be *suggested* that the use of a different research methodology could be capable of producing different results.'

which may be the case, or may not. If it's a case you particularly want to make, you can always go on to describe exactly *which* research methods might have been more appropriate. At one and the same time you're informing the reader of an important point and avoiding tearing someone else up for rags. This might strike you as being nothing more than excessive politeness, but we can bear in mind that the main business at hand is to remain objective and evaluate, not judge. Again:

Instead of: 'Any right-thinking individual can see that Professor McDaft's ideas are founded on little more than supposition and outright invention.'

This becomes: 'It might be *argued* that without extensive further study and rigorous investigation, the available grounds for support of Professor McDaft's ideas are less than complete.'

where you're making very pertinent remarks about the quality of the good Professor's output, but still doing so *without* claiming any special 'truth' for your own.

By this time, you might be thinking that an appropriate academic writing style – cool, calm and finicky in the extreme about facts and details – is productive only of dry and unexciting prose. Well, yes, you're right. The theories, concepts, ideas and research findings which are described by the prose might be wildly exciting, but the method of their description must retain as high a degree of neutrality as the writer can achieve. Only in this way can the information be given the chance to speak for itself. One last example:

Instead of: 'We are astounded to discover that every single one of the subjects to whom we administered the remedy experienced a complete absence of any and every symptom within a very short time. From this and many other types of proof, we were forced to conclude that we had indeed found a certain and 100 per cent effective cure for the common cold!'

This becomes: 'The available data on this very small sample of two subjects appears to suggest that some of the symptoms they experienced may have been alleviated to some extent by the administration of Formula A1. Detailed and extensive further study is recommended.'

Juxtaposition of information The construction of your Review notes will already have pointed you towards the possible correspondences that might exist amid your collected information. How you present these correspondences in your Review though, is a matter for careful thought. Your first priority is to be 'fair' to each and every piece of data you will use, ensuring that original messages are not in any way changed by the associations that may be made. This calls for the application of a rigorous scrutiny to whatever you write that attempts to exhibit correspondences, no matter how plain and 'simple', or how 'widely-accepted' these may seem to be. We can deal with this 'juxtaposition' under two convenient headings – Convergence and Divergence.

Convergence   Here, two or more pieces of data appear to be in 'agreement' about something, or at least are not either contradictory or mutually exclusive, and seem to be dealing with the same, or highly similar, subject. You're quite correct, that *is* a sentence written with caution in mind rather than simplicity, and I would strongly recommend that you adopt a similar outlook when you come to decide the nature of the correspondences you believe you have identified. Data from different sources may appear to say the same thing, so that one item supports another, one may even seem like a paraphrase of the other, but in writing your Review you may wish to reasonably *establish* a connection between the two in a particular way, so you must proceed with great care, remembering that you probably do not know all there is to know about either datum, and a wider knowledge base might provide you with a different perspective on the material.

So, alive to the possibilities and pitfalls, we can pass on and examine two categories of convergence.

Single points.   With the presentation in your Review of a single, specific point, it may be referenced with a single, specific source or supported by several, depending on a number of factors, such as the level of importance generally ascribed to it in the literature, or it may be viewed as being a fundamental and indispensable component in the body of knowledge. For example:

> '. . . and McMahon (1993) has suggested that quality assurance in health care services must include the routine implementation of clinical audit activity.'
> '. . . and where McMahon (1993) suggests that quality assurance in health care services must include the routine implementation of clinical audit activity, this view is shared by other authors in the field (Miriam, 1993: Winters, 1993: Harley & McGeoch, 1994).'

Where a single point is raised upon which two or more authors seem to agree, bear in mind that while 'showing' a correspondence, you must be very careful to finish off the relevant passage with no further comment from yourself that might seem to reflect one or more of the authors' views:

'The first study by Scott (1937) was widely accepted by her contemporaries, and later studies (Ratchett, 1958; Ball & Cheyne, 1963; Spinner *et al.*, 1974) have suggested that Scott's original work remained valid *and has not been superseded in any way.*'

In this setting your remarks (in italic type) are directly ascribed to every author named in the second group. Innocent as your intention might be, you can't express a judgment like this and cloak it with the mantle of another authority. Be wary of tacking on remarks that might (even subtly) be taken as a continuation of the referenced report of someone else's work. In this example, where authors have noted a continued degree of validity for earlier work, *that*'s what should be said, that and no more. You might feel that 'rounding off' the last sentence with a little semantic flourish does no harm, but it does; it imports a higher degree of validity to Scott's work by making it superlative; and except for you, nobody said that.

Doubleplus points. Orwellian overtones aside, handling two or more related points referenced by a number of authors' work can be reasonably straightforward in 'converging' material:

'In his work on auditing health services, McMahon (1994a; 1994b) has acknowledged the clinical audit guidelines produced by Balti (1991) as being of great value, a view shared by other authors in the field of quality assurance (Jackson, 1991; Nan, 1991; Wells, 1992; Wolf *et al.*, 1993; Young, 1993).

although problems can still arise:

'Bolting (1976) notes an apparent discrepancy between the research findings reported by Johnson (1975) and three of the conclusions Johnson based on that research. Other authors have supported these points (Freeman, 1975; Harris & Tweed, 1976).

So what exactly is it that Freeman, Harris and Tweed actually support – Bolting's point of view about a 'discrepancy' or Johnson's 'conclusions'? Rewriting will make it clearer and draw the 'support' troops into the proper lines:

'The conclusions made by Johnson (1975) on his research findings have been questioned on three counts by Bolting (1976), an approach shared by other authors (Freeman, 1975; Harris & Tweed, 1976).'

You can see that, no matter how *complex* your use of references might seem, it should never be too *complicated* to use them accurately, so long as your grasp and expression of the underlying issues are clear. Once you know exactly what you're trying to say, correct references may be slotted into the text appropriately.

Divergence

Diverging opinions, which can range from minor quibbles about trivia to full-blown total disagreement about fundamentals, must be represented with extreme care. It might be said that since the presentation of the **divergence of opinion in your writing lies at the heart of a balanced** Review, the need for caution and extreme accuracy will never be stronger. Presenting data from different sources that deal with the same subject while arriving at differing opinions and drawing different conclusions requires great circumspection; the results must inform the reader of the available variety of perspectives without misdirection or the least hint of your 'taking sides'.

First, we should begin with a brief examination of the possible backgrounds from which divergent material may spring.

Personal investigation   Where an author has conducted some personal activity in acquiring and handling information that is eventually published, perhaps by preparing a Literature Review or carrying out some piece of experimental (or other) study.

'Expert' knowledge base   Where an individual, steeped in the subject, provides a personal perspective on it, perhaps in the form of a critique of particular work done, or a commentary on general issues pertinent to the whole field.

Indignant self-interest   Where righteousness and protectionism drive an individual to storm into print, declaring this and declaiming that, usually with a fine disregard for 'truth'.

The first two of these, in the order given, are the 'best' bases for learning about the subject and exploring how divergent data is handled. The last, most examples of which are instantly recognisable for what they are, can still be learned from, although very seldom used as reference material: informed, considered opinion is one thing, baseless raving is quite another. If you don't think that indignant self-interest finds its way into academic literature, just keep your eyes peeled over the next few years and see who's trying to inform you about something and who's trying to convince you of something else.

Single points. As before with this raising of a single item, a single reference may be made to another author's work or, given a weighty point, several sources of salient data may be referred to:

> 'While McMahon (1993) has suggested that regular clinical audit activity is an integral part of any quality assurance programme in health care, Meddler (1991) claims that routine data collection as a result of clinical audits seldom serves any purpose in improving health care.'

Here, there is a correspondence between both authors' work; even though McMahon's 'championship' of clinical audit is not strictly refuted by Meddler, there is a reasonable point to be made in displaying a divergence of opinion. A sharper light could be thrown on the issue by demonstrating a wider perspective on the field:

> 'In a small-scale non-experimental survey, Meddler (1991) concluded that the routine data collection performed in clinical audits seldom served any purpose in improving health care, although McMahon (1993) has suggested that regular clinical audit acitvity is an integral part of any health care quality assurance programme, a view shared by other authors in the field (Ratchet, 1991; Spinner *et al.*, 1992; Ball & Cheyne, 1993).'

and this example supplies McMahon's perspective with support. There are still reservations that might be expressed, however. In displaying one viewpoint in relation to another, a contrast is made between them, but is enough data provided so as to allow the reader some yardstick for *comparison*? Meddler, after all, is spoken of as having conducted some research, as having constructed some basis for his conclusions – McMahon and company are spoken of as having a common viewpoint, but based on what: strongly held beliefs? wishful thinking? or have they too arrived at their opinions via research activity? For example:

> 'In a small-scale non-experimental survey, Meddler (1991) concluded that the routine data collection performed in clinical audits seldom served any purpose in improving health care. However, McMahon

(1993) reported after a three-year longitudinal study, conducted in a total of sixteen clinical areas across four District General Hospitals, that routine clinical audit results were instrumental in producing improved health care, a finding reported by other authors (Ratchet, 1991; Spinner *et al.*, 1992).'

where Ball and Cheyne have been left off since their opinions were not based on research. That still leaves poor Meddler as a nut being smashed by sledgehammers, of course. Are we displaying some shades of self-interest here? Are we really presenting a 'true' picture of the field, or sliding into a sales pitch? If the available literature has more and 'better' examples of Meddler's point of view, especially where these may approximate the extensive scope of McMahon's work, then we are obliged in the interests of the Review to present these. This depends on the degree of rigour brought to the literature search, but if 'contrary' material is available it mustn't be repressed, but dealt with even-handedly.

The same point dealt with in convergence about glueing on personal remarks which might be construed as stemming from a source external to the Review applies here equally to divergent opinion.

Doubleplus points. This can be a tricky business. First, here's how not to approach it:

'The flawed research methodology which Delilah (1988) ascribed to Dickens (1987) and his work on '1' was followed by suggestions that the nature of '1' had not been fully established (McCann, 1988; Walton, 1989). Moreover, it was suggested that not only was this the case, but it was also influential in the Simpson and Cole (1992) study, which attempted to replicate the findings of '1' + '1' = '2', which Dickens *et al.* (1991) had reported for their clinical trial, but could not.'

where the messages are disordered by more than poor syntax: the putative links or relationships between one point and another are cloudy and inexact, and some very shaky statements are made which indicate correspondences that probably don't exist – the work of McCann and Walton 'following' that of Delilah for example, which may have occurred in *time* but not as a *result* of Delilah's work. This point is stressed because the imputed 'relationship' accords a linear progression of opinion that runs counter to that of Dickens, and delivers a false message. With a bit of care and attention, it can all be rewritten to deliver a clearer and 'fairer' message, one that is a good deal more representative of the original work included:

'The clinical trial conducted by Dickens *et al.* (1991) suggested that '1' + '1' = '2', a finding that Simpson and Cole (1991) could not replicate in their study, further noting that the nature of '1' had not been fully established in earlier work by Dickens (1987), a view also expressed by McCann (1988) and Walton (1989). A critique by Delilah (1988) suggested that preliminary work by Dickens (1987) on the nature of '1' was flawed to an unknown degree by the use of inappropriate research methodology.'

which is much nearer the mark, although 'fully established' and 'a view also expressed' both describe perceptions which must accurately reflect the original sources.

A fairly easy mistake to make in handling doubleplus point material in divergence is to stray from one item to another without pause, and in doing so inadvertently link points in ways which you do not intend. For example:

'Morrison's seminal text "The Principles of Partying" (1983) was described by Dullard (1984) as being without foundation while Franks (1985) commented that it was "misleading".'

Here, where the original intention was to show Dullard at odds with Morrison and Franks at odds with Dullard's interpretation of Morrison, a reader might receive the impression that Franks agrees with Dullard and both are at odds with Morrison.

Again, the best grip you can achieve on understanding the material provides you with the best base for representing it clearly.

Discussion

Your discussion of the information presented should be brief, lucid and pertinent. While the 'discussion' is rightly the place for you as the author to 'appear' – making summary comments, perhaps pointing up an issue or two – the contents should never stray from the writing style 'ideals': accuracy in the presentation of information and objectivity in handling it. A few guidelines will help.

1. There can be a great temptation in Discussions to continue scattering references around, shoring up your remarks and lending weight to pronouncements, but really there's no need for this, for good reason. Your remarks should be based on the material which has already been fully explained and referenced, in which case your reader should be in

possession of that which he or she should know in order to evaluate what you say; your pronouncements should be completely germane to the topic and should be cool, detached and the clear result of the application of balanced reasoning.

A Literature Review Discussion is not the place to 'prove' anything, nor is it a platform from which to harangue the assembled readership. Because of the effort you've made to construct the Review, the Discussion might be seen as a small (a very small) shop window, where you put some thoughts and ideas on display which the reader may or may not choose to buy, a decision which you shouldn't try to influence by embarking on a feverish and distracting sales pitch.

A reader comes to a Review with the expectation of learning what a number of authors have to say about a particular subject. That includes you, but you're last on the list, and the expectation made of you is that your authorship will be calm, rational, and informative without seeking to be didactic.

2. Don't introduce new data into your Discussion. Besides being sneaky, it's apt to produce an ambivalent message; you don't have the elbow room to explore issues at length in a Discussion, and the fact that you've chosen to highlight some aspect of the topic in this way can make it look like a personal 'value' choice and an attempt to influence the reader. Stick rigidly to the material contained in the data presentation and exposition.

3. The tenor of your Discussion may set you down gently on one side of the topic fence or the other, especially if the Review deals with a subject on which opinion is strongly divided or in some other way lends itself to contention rather than cool debate. This 'taking of sides' can be almost impossible to eradicate from your Discussion, but it should never be evident in the rest of the Review. So long as accuracy and objectivity are strictly observed, you have earned the right to express an opinion, but be sure to express it in sensible, guarded terms. The purposes of your Review are many, but an important one of them is to deliver information and encourage learning – which is not best served if your reader trawls up to your Discussion only to find you raving there about who's right and who's abysmally wrong.

The careful language of academia comes to your aid here, and prefacing your personal statements with well-chosen safety shields is more likely to keep your reader reading and understanding – so an idea might be 'suggested', a viewpoint might be presented as 'one of many possible' outlooks, and if you can't restrain yourself from saying something that might provoke screaming outrage, it might be neutralised a little by presenting it as a 'potential consequence' of a 'partisan attachment' to an idea 'whose limits should be explored in the best interests of this important subject'.

It's safer not to slip into semantic machinations like this, of course. Your Discussion should illuminate a topic, not espouse a cause. You should come across as a thoughtful individual willing to consider any and every view, not as an academic guerilla.

4. Finding yourself on the brink of preparing your Discussion can be a heady experience. The bulk of your efforts lies behind you and a rush of learning to the head can seduce you into assuming an attitude of omniscience. As a result, your Discussion transforms itself from a brief commentary into a lengthy treatise jammed to the brim with Olympian judgments – for which you have few grounds and even less justification.

   Handling a Discussion in this way might seem like something you just wouldn't do. If you're certain about that, convinced that you won't cross the boundary between 'learner learning' and 'learned expounding', all well and good. If, however, you even suspect that the temptation to chatter on *ad infinitum* will prove irresistible, be prepared to draft and redraft your Discussion, be prepared to prune away all of the 'interesting' little diversions that take you away from the heart of the matter, be prepared to brutally dump any and all material that threatens to extend the Discussion beyond the margins of conciseness and precision.

5. Lastly, a very simple point: write your Discussion after the rest of the Review is in its final draft, including the Abstract, and check it with care. Try hard not to 'read between the lines' of the Discussion, mentally filling in any gaps in information that should be present to explain and underpin what you're saying. Be sure that any rounding-up of material is justified and that the rounding-off of the Discussion is plain and simple.

Context

While observing the requirements that may be expected of you by your assessors with regard to the presentation of the Review, and while considering the details of the Review framework provided here, you can still be at a loss in knowing how to handle the basic mechanics of fitting data together – which bit goes where, and why. Now, it's hardly a secret between us that a fair amount of the material dealt with under 'Framework' handled information with a strong regard for finding an appropriate context in which to present it. We might name this as an 'internal' context, where the components of your text are woven together in order to represent a line of thoughts and ideas for the reader to follow. However, the substance of your Review itself has to fit into a wider context, as a package of information which represents a wider body of knowledge; it should be derived reasonably from, and at the same time take its place within, an 'external' context which serves to guide and underline the contents of the Review and the way in which they are presented.

This all sounds rather complicated and a bit abstract, and I won't mislead you by saying that *every* Review topic automatically lends itself to being explored in the ways noted below, but the business of imposing an 'external' context on your Review can be reduced to a straightforward search for, and logical ordering of, contextual 'milestones' and 'signposts' in the information pool obtained from your Review material.

Signposts and milestones

First, a general pointer: the ways of grouping information noted here are not meant to be construed as being mutually exclusive. A mixture of them can provide a very logical and sequential route through the literature, with just as much utility as that afforded by a single unifying context. It all depends on what you find in the material under scrutiny: the suitability of which for being handled in a particular way or ways will determine the method you choose. So, if you discover that the usefulness of any grouping applies only to a portion of the data, cast around for another one and see if a series of contexts can be identified and used appropriately.

Chronology   This is the easiest of contexts to handle. If the subject permits it, data can either be taken from one item to another in a linear progression, or one aspect of the topic can be pursued to a conclusion before the focus of the Review returns to an earlier time to isolate, identify and explain another strand of the material. The point is that the underlying theme of the context is the concept of the passage of time, which you can justifiably assume is already in your reader's grasp without needing to be explained.

Review topics which address the historical development of a subject are obvious choices for this context, but a wide range of topics can benefit from it – usually delivered in potted versions at the beginning or end of the data presentation. 'Milestones' occurring in a body of knowledge are fairly easy to identify and place in an appropriate chronological context – 'The invention of rubber gloves in 18— prompted the Edinburgh surgeon MacKnife . . .', 'The discovery of the bacterium "Idlin malenurssii" in 1973 caused a revolution in work practices . . .'. A great deal of information can be 'hooked' into place in a chronological order which delivers a series of pertinent milestones, whatever their nature might be.

Concepts   Here, singular concepts embedded in the subject can be selected out to be used on their own or in combination to provide 'signposts' for sequencing and presenting data. For example, a Review topic concerned with the prevention of pressure sores in people made bedfast post-operatively might deal consecutively with the 'context concepts' of skin hygiene, good nutrition, maintenance of peripheral circulation, positional changes and so on in a step-by-step exploration of the available literature. Not all material lends itself to being ordered in this way, though. Sometimes, a single 'all-encompassing' concept must be closely examined as a whole and the most convenient signposts to use may be identified in terms of what 'expert' and 'authoritative' sources declare to be its most important characteristics. Take 'Nursing' as an example of this kind of concept, where with a prolonged trek through the literature with the topic of 'The contribution of nursing to modern health care' as a suitably catch-all Review title in mind, you might grow increasingly frustrated at an apparent absence of any agreed definition of what nursing actually *is*, never mind how any contributions to health care might be positively identified. What you *will* find are what might be described as 'concept features' which, taken individually and together, are probably in most people's lexicons when they discuss the nature of nursing – 'nurture', 'support', 'empathy', 'compassion', 'practical', 'organised', 'professional', 'research-based'. All of these (and more) can be used as the signposts for the Review, when relevant material may be associated in a series of issues which are characteristic of the underlying concept.

With no other starting point to use as a springboard, the identification, isolation and selection of appropriate concepts in ordering your Review can seem a little difficult at first. It becomes easier with practice, though, and you can bear in mind that you're calling on a fair amount of brainpower here, so go easy on yourself at your first attempts.

Chalk and cheese   In some fields the expression of 'expert' opinions may be quite rigidly polarised, a situation which offers a ready-made external context which is no less useful because it stems from people's perceptions rather than any inherent property of the subject itself. The main task in this case is to find and order the central issues which serve as the sources for division in the field and present these with an even distribution of material both 'for' and 'against' each item raised. For example, with a Review topic like this:

'The occupation by men of senior management posts in nursing'

a number of possibilities in choosing an external context are available, such as a chronicle of events detailing different employing authorities' 'track record' in recruiting and deploying men in nursing service management. However, a much more fruitful line of enquiry might be found in pursuing how people perceive the whole issue, and in drawing out some central issues with which to illuminate the topic. For instance:

- All else being equal, such as qualifications and relevant experience, are men viewed any differently from women by prospective employers?

- Do men in nursing receive more support and encouragement from local hierarchies to seek promotion than do their female colleagues?

- Are men selectively prepared for promotion into senior posts by being given a readier access to training opportunities than most female nurses?

- In a profession predominantly peopled by women, why do so many men occupy senior management posts – to a degree which is out of all proportion to their number in nursing?

You can see that while the named subject is 'real' and may be dealt with in a variety of ways, a host of fundamental issues may clamour for attention when once the exploration of personal perspectives is begun: perspectives which can quickly circumscribe a relevant external context.

It's worth repeating that your choice of context depends greatly on the nature of the material, and your understanding of *that* will come about over time as you consider the literature at length.

References

Whatever referencing system you use in your Review, make sure that you use it correctly and with complete accuracy. By the time you've finished writing it, you might (we're only human) be sick of the sight of every page. On the other hand, you might be seriously impressed with the slick piece of academic brilliance you've turned out. Whichever emotional state you find yourself in – don't be reluctant to check and check again that every single reference is in its correct place in the text *and* included (in the right order) in the reference list. These issues are always important when you're writing for a reader, but never more so than when the foundations of a Literature Review are concerned.

EXERCISES

1. **(a)** Construct two Literature Review titles; base one of them on a subject currently to the fore in professional journals and one of them on a special professional interest of your own. Carry out a preliminary literature search for each of them and select six information sources for each – try to include material from different types of sources: textbook, research paper, critique and so on.
   (b) Prepare a set of Review notes for each subject; make them as detailed as you can.
   (c) Using these notes, write at least two paragraphs on each subject which deal with suitably referenced items of information.
2. **(a)** Using 'convergent' data from at least four different sources, write a single paragraph dealing with just one item of information. Include as many pertinent references as you can.
   (b) Using the same data sources write two paragraphs – each of them dealing with at least two items of information which are as fully referenced as you can manage with the material to hand. Keep these paragraphs as brief as possible.
3. Repeat Exercise **2**, only using 'divergent' data this time.
4. Choose a subject about which you are knowledgeable and search the literature for several examples of relevant material dealt with in either Literature Reviews or research papers. DON'T read the abstracts.

   Select at least one Review or paper, preferably the most straightforward. Read it through several times, make notes, consider it at length until you think you've got a good grasp of the contents. Now, write two versions of an abstract for the data: the first can be reasonably lengthy, the second should be as succinct as you can make it.

   Compare both versions with what the author of the original abstract had to say. If what you've written is wide of the mark in this comparison, redraft whichever version was *nearest to the original in meaning and detail* until it fairly represents the author's abstract. Note which inclusions or exclusions of data from your writing are needed in order to expand or trim your version.
5. Construct an 'external context' for each of the sample Review titles noted below:

   'The implementation of Primary Nursing in hospital-based health care'
   'The development of community-based mental health nursing services'
   'Patient involvement in care planning: reality or myth?'
   'Practitioners' perspectives on research-based practice in nursing'

6 Preparing for examinations

As a learner, you've probably reached the conclusion that educational courses are all about passing exams. In your cooler moments you know that's not so, you're in the business of learning, of participating in your education. Exams are only a part of that process. An important part, yes, but only part of the whole.

That said, here's how you treat exams as an *integral* part of the whole.

KNOW YOUR COURSE

There is no substitute for knowing and understanding exactly what your course requires of you in terms of 'proof of learning'. You should assemble a detailed knowledge of which type of assessments will be made of your 'learning performance' and when. For our purposes here, the chief among these assessments will be any written examinations you will take. Find out the schedule of exams set for every part of your course, get hold of past papers and familiarise yourself with how they're laid out. Pay no attention to the contents of the questions at this stage – you'll only upset yourself. In short, acquaint yourself with exams as a fact of life. Deal head on with their reality for you as a learner, let all the fear and trembling rise up, confront it, then pass on. The vast majority of us allow exams to become a bane in our lives usually because we put off thinking about them until the last possible moment. With this delaying tactic comes a frame of mind that fails to perceive exams for what they are – tests of learning – and makes of them instead insurmountable obstacles set in a deadly game of chance.

Let's be frank here; most of the people who have already taken the exams you face now were successful. For a simple reason – the contents of exams are drawn from course material. In other words, if you participate in your course, make the effort to learn, do what's required of you – how can you fail? You're not going to revise one body of knowledge only to be asked questions about another one.

Don't let the notion of exams transform itself until it paralyses you with anxiety, especially if you face 'Final' exams at some point in your learning. Accept them for what they are and prepare for them from the beginning in accordance with their true nature – reasoned and reasonable enquiries into your learning.

Essentially, any 'preparation for exams' is a way of identifying, organising and acquiring the knowledge you are expected to possess about course material. So the first place to start is by clearly identifying a set of course messages and course targets that will underpin your understanding of what you should be about.

COURSE MESSAGES AND COURSE TARGETS

Every course is 'sectioned off' in some way, with subject material slotted in to the overall time available. This is the result of planning, so that some subjects are taught from the ground up through a succession of 'levels' in order for the learner to develop an appropriate knowledge base, or to allow a group of related subjects to be linked and taught together.

Whatever the reason might be, you can make it evident and understand it by doing the following:

1. Take a detailed syllabus for your course and follow each subject through the detailed schedule arranged for it. Note where specific subjects are introduced and when, and note how varied subjects are linked. Compare these notes with the current exam timetable. Plot, as accurately as you can, when 'sections' or stages of the course are examined.
2. Gather together every exam paper set for each 'section' of the course over the past three years. Note, in broad headings, the subjects examined, together with an indication of the 'depth' of knowledge expected. You're not looking for anything else here, certainly not in the way of 'guessing' what your own exams will contain. You're just trying to piece together an understanding of the nature of the exams.
3. Compare your syllabus 'plot' with the notes you made about exams, and consider how they relate to each other. The point about this is to give you practice in 'seeing' how the syllabus and the exam contents fit together.

    Without going into too much detail, try to form a picture of how each subject, or set of subjects, is examined, and why. In essence, what you're trying to derive here is an understanding of the Aims and Objectives of your course as these relate to the function of examinations.

4. Try this understanding out on a teacher. Make it clear that your intention in doing so is to grasp the core purposes of the course, *not* to define 'important' and 'trivial' topics, and somehow 'pre-select' them for grades of effort.

Having done all this, you should be closer to a reasonably detailed overview of the course, and the shape of course messages and targets should be forming in your mind. Keep them there, and clothe them out more fully as you progress, maintaining an awareness of the markers and milestones you reach as the course goes on. Following any course of education is made easier if you know the route you are to follow and recognise the value of making and using a map where X marks an examination spot.

Forgive me stating the obvious, but the person who will take your exams is you. Not a 'special' you, a 'new' you, who will somehow come into being just before the exams are due. You. The you that you are. Now is the time for you to find out a little more about the person you'll rely on to pass those exams.

DIAGNOSING PERSONAL STRENGTHS AND WEAKNESSES

How realistic are you when it comes to self-appraisal? and how fair is it to ask you a question like that? Not very, but it's necessary. You have to spend some time considering how 'fit' you are as a learner who will take exams. Start by asking yourself some questions:

- Do you study regularly?
- Do you study effectively and test your learning?
- Is your learning important to you?
- Are you willing to make every necessary effort to succeed in your learning?

The first two of these questions are about your behaviour and the last two are about your attitudes, but all four of them are vital components in successful learning. Get these issues straight in your head and then use them as yardsticks in assessing other personal attitudes and behaviour that will have a bearing on how you participate in your course. You have to make a commitment to learning, and be prepared to order your personal priorities to fit the demands of your course.

So be brutally honest with yourself – if a willingness to learn and a capacity for study are essential, how reluctant are you to hit the books? If you find a subject difficult, how many excuses can you make up to explain away your avoidance of it? Are you congenitally slothful or do waves of inertia overcome you only when there's any studying to be done? Are you a self-starter or do you need lots of encouragement? Is work well done its own reward or do you prefer instant recognition and rounds of applause? If all your exams were dumped from the course tomorrow, would you do any work at all? What value do you put on your learning, and what price are you willing to pay for it?

This attempt to clarify some areas of self-knowledge is important. Being fully aware of your personal attributes and how these might affect your learning allows you to build on your strengths and remedy your weaknesses. In time, and by paying close attention to the results of personally set or 'external' assessments, you will come to acquire an appreciation of the level of your knowledge, but the acquisition of this knowledge can be seriously affected by the depth of ignorance you retain about yourself as a learner. Correcting that ignorance is the first step to ensuring you will succeed, because it centres on finding and putting a name to any deficits in attitude and behaviour that serve to create obstacles between you and your learning. No matter how uncomfortable this process might prove to be, it's worth it.

Don't waste a second in comparing yourself to other people. It's pointless. Besides, you'd probably pick a genius and only end up aggravating yourself.

Now for the meat of exam preparation. Start on the first day of your course. Handle the information you acquire today as though you were about to be examined on it tomorrow. Does that sound excessive? Perhaps because you think of exams as occurring some time in the dim and distant future? Whereas, in actual fact, they're nearer than the door. Time passes. Start as you mean to go on.

LEARNING AND RELEARNING

Think of the amount of effort you might put into acquiring a knowledge of any subject. Now double it, and don't be too concerned if you have to revise this figure upwards as time goes by. Learning anything takes time, and never forget that without *rehearsal* and *use*, those indispensable channel-diggers of memory, a thing learned can be forgotten. If you can't recall it, you'll have to relearn it.

Don't be a miser with learning time. Covet all information that comes your way and immerse yourself in it. Go over new material again and again, make connections with what you already know. Think, write and speak about it. Don't fiddle with it, *handle* it until you know it well. Don't put a subject down, in any sense; everything presented on your course should be considered as grist to the mill.

At any given moment in your course, the introduction of a new subject, or a marked step up in the level of an 'old' subject, can threaten to fixate your attention to the exclusion of everything else. Be wary; calculate your time well and accord everything a place. Including the following.

Revision

Let no gains in knowledge die through neglect. The most hard-won material can wither on the vine if it isn't fed some attention. Plan to revise everything you've learned. Don't faint. Well-grounded learning can be revised with just a little effort that more than repays the energy expended. The basis of this revision can be rooted in the preparation of a series of 'learning digests'.

These 'digests' are texts which summarise the notes you prepare from textbooks and lectures. They act as 'synopses' for all the ground you cover in writing out accurate and comprehensive notes on course material, and they can be used as informative 'refreshers' which reduce the time needed for revising and relearning.

Here's how to prepare one

1. Select a topic and gather together all the relevant notes you have on it. Make sure these are thorough and well-prepared. If you've skimped anything, or you need to bring some details up-to-date, do it now.
2. Divide your notes up into sections, ordered in a logical sequence derived from the nature of the subject material.
3. Take each section in turn and compose a precis of the information contained in every page – use single words and short headings wherever you can, otherwise keep sentences strictly to the point and very brief – you're the only one who's going to read this, so don't worry about grammar or how it looks; if it's clear to you, that's all you need.

   If your notes contain equations or formulae, write these out in full. If tables or diagrams are included, just record, for example, 'Table for . . . ' and note the purpose. Don't recreate the graphic in the precis.
4. Squeeze as much information as clarity will allow on each page of this precis and continue until each division of your notes has been condensed. Now very carefully compare the contents of notes and

precis, making certain that you have faithfully and accurately transcribed the outline of the original material.

5. Now read through each section of your notes, then read the appropriate precis. As you do so, call to mind the details contained in your notes as you read the appropriate 'cue' word, heading or sentence. Visualise any tables and diagrams when you read their names. Does your precis offer you good enough 'cues' which prompt your recall of the material? If not, round it out with a few extra items until you can proceed through it with the certainty that you're missing nothing.

6. Build up a complete record of all your notes in this precis form, and keep them current with the material you add to the original notes. With practice, you'll find that as you write new notes, the shape of their eventual precis will begin to take shape at the same time.

7. If you find you're a dab hand at creating precis, and you become convinced that you know and understand all of the information they represent, a word of warning: DON'T be tempted to discard your notes.

Once your 'digests' are made, keep them with the original notes, and read both through together on a regular basis. On the first few occasions you do this, begin with the notes. As you become increasingly familiar with the material, read the precis and then the notes. What you're working towards is an ease of recall where related information is prompted just by scanning the precis. In essence, the precis becomes an 'Index' to your notes.

This takes time and practice, so start early.

Discussions and Consultations with Experts and Others

So far we've had you pointed at the books, studying hard and acquiring knowledge, but you can't carry notes into an exam. It's just you and the paper. What's inside your head will have to suffice. In which case, you have to be reasonably sure that your portable knowledge *is* sufficient, not only the bare bones of it, but in how you'll make the skeleton get up and walk around. That takes the ability to handle information appropriately. The best way to sharpen this ability is through discussing information with other people. For example:

1. Take every opportunity to verify, increase and refine the knowledge you acquire by talking it over with experts. State your understanding of a subject in your own words, define concepts, explore ideas, quote facts and figures. Ask them plainly if you've got it right, ask them to correct you if you're wrong. If they bring a new shade of meaning to what you

know, paraphrase what they say and feed it back to them for comment. Never pass up the chance to mould some information in your head by speaking it aloud and making messages with it. How those messages are received and acted upon by other, more knowledgeable, people can provide first-class opportunities for investigating the quantity and quality of your learning.

2. Join discussion groups on your course, or start one: have a meeting at least once a week where half-a-dozen of you sit down to chew through a topic or two. Make sure you gather like-minded souls who *want* to speak and listen. Each meeting should last for an hour or so and everyone should have their say, most especially you. Take notes. Afterwards, check these against good sources.

The whole idea about discussing learning material is that you're obliged to think about it, to sort it out and organise it in order to speak about it and make sense. You're bringing your cognitive abilities into play and laying down well-rehearsed memories that you are willing and able to recall and use. When you sit down to an exam, that's all you have to rely on, so making it fit for the purpose will serve you well.

The recommendations made so far obviously involve the use of considerable time. As exam dates draw near you need to start rethinking and replanning your study time – increasing it if possible? – but certainly, managing it well.

Time Management

1. What time is available to you? What time must be given over to all your other daily activities? What time is left – on a daily, weekly and monthly basis? Work it out on paper, write down the results.

2. Parcel this time out in a schedule that allows space for all the subjects you must 'complete' your learning in and which you must revise. Write this schedule out so that all subjects are represented in both learning and revision time. Build in some slack to every week's worth of study time to allow for some manoeuvring – to permit last-minute changes and reshuffles, NOT for ditching the books and wandering off.

Some people can study the same subject for hours at a stretch. Others find an hour at any subject torture. Most of us are somewhere in between, and our attention span is governed by whether we find the topic particularly interesting or view it as very important. Set allotted time spans for each subject as sensibly as you can, considering *volume of work* as the prime deciding factor, then break up the overall time into study periods you find most productive. It might be that you find 45–60 minutes spent studying any subject is the maximum you can give it before your concentration slips, but moving onto another subject gives you a fresh impetus to spend another hour learning. And so on. Whatever size these chunks of subject study time prove to be, you can use them to good effect.

3. Stick to your schedule, work within it and make it work for you. If, for any reason, you can't follow your schedule for a while, get back into it as soon as you can and rejig the time remaining to make up for the lost study time.

4. Study wisely and study well, but don't study to exhaustion. This is the one and only time I will mention your health in relation to your work programme as a learner, and I raise the issue here because the time before examinations is when you are likely to work hardest. You might have a mountain of work to get through, and it can be very easy to forget to rest, eat and sleep enough to maintain your mental and physical health in a reasonable state of repair.

No one expects you to study yourself into the ground. Courses are spread over time; make sure you do the same with your learning. Prepare early. Don't concentrate exclusively on your studies. Don't forget to talk to your family and friends, go to the movies, put your feet up and blank out for a while. Don't be a stranger to your bed; if you're fit you can probably do without sufficient sleep for a while, but eventually you'll end up doing your thinking with four pounds of cotton wool stuffed into your skull. Eat properly, stop munching snacks on the run – if every book you open has crumbs in it, you're playing hell with your physiology; your body will be underfed while your brain is out to lunch. Take care of yourself, you're the only you you've got.

Besides, people who wreck themselves for exams usually go on to wreck the exams.

YARDSTICKS FOR PERFORMANCE

As you're working and preparing for exams, you should keep a regular check on the level and quality of the information at your disposal *and* find out if you're handling it appropriately. This calls for a process of assessment. You will have made a good beginning towards self-assessment by participating in discussions intended to provide a personal feedback with which you can examine your knowledge base. There are other avenues open to you, some more formal than others.

1. Make an easy start by ending every study period with jotting down a brief summary of what you've been reading. It needn't be too detailed, just accurate. Try writing a single page outline of material just covered, then check it against your notes. If you've made any mistakes, either in fact or in the sequential presentation of information, correct these from your notes. Read your outline aloud. Keep it until you make another one at the next study period for the same subject, then compare the two. Your grasp of the material should show improvement on how you handle the material and in how much you can recall.

2. When you think you know and understand subject material, ask an obliging friend to ask you questions from your notes, someone who doesn't know the material and won't be tempted to qualify or discuss your answers in any way – *they* aren't assessing the nature of your responses, *you* are. Have them scan through your notes and pick points at random as bases for simple questions, such as 'What does "X" mean?' 'Is "Y" important?' 'Where does "Z" fit into what you know about this subject?'

   Jot down the issues raised by these questions and record your responses, *after* you've said them. Check them out later for accuracy and comprehensiveness.

3. Take a recent paper set for your exam and select two questions from it: one that deals with your 'weakest' subject and one to which you feel fairly confident about being able to make a good response.

   (a) Take the first and answer it in a script without putting any time limit on how long it takes you. Continue until you feel you've dealt with it as best you can. Now do the same thing again, only this time work from your notes and set down what you consider would be a 'model' answer. Ask a teacher to review them both: not necessarily to mark them, but to give you comments on how appropriate the responses are. You will already have a fair idea of the difference in quality between the 'model' answer and your first attempt, but what you're trying to establish here is whether the 'model' answer can in fact be used as a realistic yardstick against which to measure the value of your first response.

   Pay very close attention to what the teacher has to say about both answers. Make a note of the comments and apply them to the scripts – look for and consider what the teacher found 'good' and 'bad' about them.

Now do the exercise again with two new questions picked from another exam. Be sure to incorporate the proof of any general advice the teacher gave on answering exam questions.

(b) Have a recent exam paper ready. Don't read the contents. Sit in a quiet room where you won't be disturbed. Now look over the paper, choose a question to which you can make a 'best' response, and answer it within the time span it could be given in a 'real' exam. Be exact about this time, don't go over it. When you're finished, whatever you feel about your script, submit it to a teacher for marking. While you're waiting to get it back, go to the books and write a 'model' answer to the question – one that could be written out within the specified time.

When your marked answer is ready, discuss it with the teacher. If you've been awarded a failing mark, get detailed instructions on what you need to know in order to fill out your knowledge base. If you've 'passed', ask how you might have improved your mark. In either case, listen with care to any comments the teacher makes.

Now, with what you've learned about how and why your script was marked as it was, make an attempt at marking your 'model' answer. It doesn't matter what the final score is, just go through it with a fine toothcomb, searching for and evaluating information that is germane to the inquiry posed by the exam question. You're not looking for big gains in information here, you're developing the ability to assess your output as a learner.

A word of advice: do this exercise no more than three or four times. It's the acquisition of the assessment skills you're after; once you've got the rudiments, you can practise them on loads of material you produce. Don't become fixated on using them only for exam answers. Develop the range and acuity of your skills by applying them elsewhere.

Being able to 'stand back' and take a (reasonably) dispassionate and (completely) rational look at your performance as a learner is a great boon. It also requires effort and a real drive to do well. Stick with it. Acquiring a degree of objectivity about your learning and the ability to weigh it in the balance is a big step to take, but one that's well worth taking.

So. Now you're reading, discussing and producing answers. All that remains is strategems, presented here in two forms – *graphics* and *mnemonics*.

Graphics

If any subject material lends itself readily to being represented in a table, diagram or some other 'pictorial' form, go ahead and put it together. Make it as striking and memorable as you can, hang all the information from it that fits there. You're giving information a definite 'shape' and that helps recall. When you've knocked your graphic into a final form, copy it out until you can do it from memory completely and accurately.

Graphics aren't a substitute for learning, of course; there's nothing magical about them. You still have to know the material, but they can provide you with a well-signposted route through a stack of information.

Related material that doesn't sit easily in a diagrammatic or tabular form might be constructed into information clusters, with the subject heading in the middle and little lines radiating out from it passing through information sequences that represent the 'natural' ordering of the material. These need to be drawn out with care and can be time-consuming to get right. Make very sure they're accurately detailed before rehearsing their reproduction in their final form. An example is given below of how you might put together a simple information cluster dealing with the human

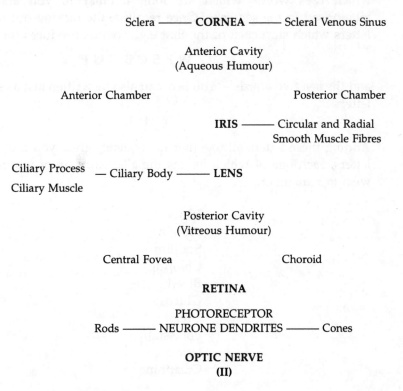

Sclera ——— **CORNEA** ——— Scleral Venous Sinus

Anterior Cavity
(Aqueous Humour)

Anterior Chamber   Posterior Chamber

IRIS ——— Circular and Radial
Smooth Muscle Fibres

Ciliary Process
                 — Ciliary Body ——— **LENS**
Ciliary Muscle

Posterior Cavity
(Vitreous Humour)

Central Fovea   Choroid

RETINA

PHOTORECEPTOR
Rods ——— NEURONE DENDRITES ——— Cones

**OPTIC NERVE
(II)**

eye – here, using a cluster shape that represents the *successive* structures encountered by light as it passes through the eye.

One last word about graphics in general: reproducing a diagram, or table, or whatever, in an exam without supplying a text that *fully* explains its content is unacceptable. Graphics should *always* be supported by appropriate, and complete, explanations.

Mnemonics

A 'mnemonic' is a memory aid, which is designed to encourage the recall of one piece of information by linking it in some way with another piece, where this last piece is much more familiar to you and easily recalled.

For example – if you wanted to remember the names of common substances found in glomerular filtrate, you could make up a little sentence of capitalised words:

'Weary People Sleep Constantly,
Being Grossly Under-Powered,
You See.'

which uses words which are long familiar to you and are easily memorised in the sentence. Once recalled, the picking out of the capital letters which start each of the first eight words produces the string:

W P S C B G U P

and the last two words – 'You See' can also be written just as single capital letters:

U C

Adding these letters all together in sequence gives you a total of 10 first letters, each one of which begins the *alternative* set of words which you wish to remember:

Water
Proteins
Sodium
Chloride
Bicarbonate
Glucose
Urea
Potassium
Uric acid
Creatinine

If you're seeing a mnemonic here for the first time, and thinking the whole business is simple-minded, you're right. That's why it works. Mnemonics can create simple 'hooks' on which you can hang much more complex information.

There's a limit to what can be done with mnemonics of course; logically ordered factual material lends itself well to the creation of mnemonics, conceptual or 'abstract' material doesn't. Whatever you use them for, bear a few points in mind.

- Make your mnemonics as personally *significant* as you can. If you like poetry, make up mnemonics in verse form. Use familiar words and phrases from a favourite sport or pastime.

- Keep mnemonics *simple*, and as *short* as possible.

- Remember to rehearse both your mnemonic and the original material *together*, so that the two *do* become linked.

7 Examinations
Essays and multiple choice questions

Most examinations on particular subjects are presented regularly in the same format and most of these formats take the shape of a series of questions requiring 'essay' type answers. There are different versions of these 'essay' examinations, and the main points of these are dealt with in some detail here, while the latter part of this chapter addresses a 'Multiple Choice' exam format.

The first thing to note, and I can't stress this enough, is that you should quickly become acquainted with the types of formal examinations that will be used as part of the assessment methodology implemented in your course. 'Past papers' will be readily available for all 'external' examinations and for many 'course-led' exams, and you should make a point of acquiring a range of these at an early date. Not, please note, so that you can start trying to guess at what might be in the exams *you* will eventually take, but so that you can familiarise yourself with the 'size and shape' of the exam itself. This is a good first step to take, especially if you're a bit apprehensive about the whole business. Professional exams are an important step in your progress as a learner, and all of us feel a natural anxiety about them. But because some exams are used as selection mechanisms for determining who will go forward with their education and who won't, or who will 'qualify' for practice in the profession and who won't, we tend to let this anxiety grow with regard to any and every examination, and sometimes end up dreading the very idea of exams. It can be a very short step to take in this perspective and go from fearful thoughts about exams to the dubious comfort of avoiding any thought about them at all – which might, in part, relieve an immediate emotion but will do nothing about ensuring that you maintain an appropriate awareness of what examinations are really about – straightforward enquiries into what you know about things you can reasonably be expected to know something about. Any examination is just a measure of how you retain and handle information. It might sometimes *feel* like a didactic inquisition from whose results your personal worth, intellectual, social and moral integrity may be held up for mocking scrutiny, but that isn't so. We just frighten ourselves with thoughts of the reality and inescapability of exams and make of them something which they are not intended to be.

Trying to engender in yourself a cool frame of mind about exams is always worthwhile. The best way to begin is by coming to grips with how they are constructed and what requirements they will make of you as a learner.

EXAMINATION RULES

Every examination paper is prefaced by a set of instructions telling you what to do in the exam. Read these carefully and obey them to the letter. Besides anything else, a thorough reading of this preface will help settle you in the first minute or two of an exam – it gives you a little practice at thinking, rather than just experiencing tension.

The instructions in the Preface will look something like this.

'Time allowed: 3 hours'

Read this and note it, check your watch and mentally mark your starting and finishing times. The exam invigilator present may give you periodic time checks throughout the exam or may not. Just make sure you're personally aware of the passage of time and how you're measuring out your efforts in accordance with the time rule. The time set for the exam is intended to allow fully detailed answers to be given to the required number of questions that should be addressed, and a small part of the intended purpose of the exam is to see how you handle your responses within the time frame.

'A total of FOUR questions must be answered'

Usually, the total number of questions to which you are expected to provide answers is about half of the available questions in the paper or thereabouts. This ensures that you're given the chance to make a selection of questions which you believe might 'best' represent your state of knowledge and ability to handle information. This selection, however, is often constrained in some way, usually by the requirement for the total number to be made up from a combination of answers to questions located in different 'sections' of the exam paper. These 'sections' are intended to reflect differing areas of knowledge upon which the questions will be based and, depending on the examiner's purposes, some may contain a single, compulsory question, while others offer a limited choice from a brief set of questions.

Make sure you know for certain how many questions you must answer and whether you can make a free selection from among the total number of questions provided, or whether any specified questions are to be answered. If the exam paper is divided into sections, supplementary instructions are usually placed at the beginning of each section to remind you of what you should do. Read these with care.

'Each question is allocated a total of 25 marks'

Twenty-five is the most common total of marks awarded to each question in professional examinations. Not invariably, but it happens often enough for us to be able to make some assumptions about the issue.

The first of these is that if exam questions accruing 25 marks are sub-divided into sections where the marks for each section are noted alongside as a fraction of the overall mark, you've been given what can prove to be a very handy ready reckoner which can guide you in the completion of a question, not only in terms of how many items of information might be included in the answer to each section, but also in terms of how concisely you can shape the overall answer. This is more readily understood by comparing the mechanics of answering a 'sectioned' question with those required where a question is stated as a whole and a 'single' answer is required for 25 marks. The first answer can be presented in a condensed, 'reporting' style, while the second requires a more formal and discursive essay-type answer.

Another reasonable assumption to make is that if an exam requires four questions to be answered, each worth 25 marks, then the 'Pass Mark' is 50. Which *is* reasonable, but might not be true. Some exam pass marks *are* 50 per cent of the total marks possible, some are less, some are more. It's perfectly legitimate for examiners to adjust the pass mark for an exam either up or down (within a reasonable margin) if their consensus of expert opinion suggests that the degree of difficulty of a particular examination justifies such an alteration. With this in mind, you can see that while assigned marks to parts of questions can be useful in answering individual questions, the *overall* result can't be taken for granted. Never, for whatever reason, be tempted to curtail an answer because you think you've done enough to accumulate a pass mark. Squeeze *every* possible mark out of *every* answer.

'Use separate answer books for each answer'

In most formal exam settings special Answer booklets are provided for your use. All have space for your name and Examination Code number and other details, and most supply a few brief instructions on how the booklet is to be used, such as writing on one side of the paper only and sticking to the margins. Read these through and abide by them.

Once you've gone over the examination rules, it's time to take your first look at the exam questions and begin the selection of those which you will answer – two activities which shouldn't take place simultaneously but often do. We'll deal with how questions are worded in a moment, but I should make an important point first:

NEVER SELECT THE QUESTIONS YOU WILL ANSWER UNTIL YOU'VE READ THROUGH AND UNDERSTOOD EVERY QUESTION CONTAINED IN THE PAPER

because a mixture of fright, trepidation and an overwhelming urge to start writing can have you scribbling your way through answer booklets without once giving the questions the attention they deserve. The traditional 'post-mortems' which candidates hold immediately after an exam are customarily enlivened by the sight of people smacking their foreheads in dismay after hearing somebody else explain just what Question X was actually about. And usually, the forehead-smackers have every right to be dismayed, because instead of spending the few extra seconds in coming to grips with the contents of Question X, they've sprinted through the entire question set at a rate that practically ensures a lack of comprehension. The point is, of course, that reading something under exam conditions can take that bit extra effort, especially when you suspect that what you're about to read is bad news for you and your knowledge base. However, it still has to be done, in as cool and rational manner as you can possibly muster: read the questions through at least twice, let their meaning sink in and *then* make your selection.

One of the easiest things to do in an exam is to provide a beautiful answer, complete in every last detail, to a question that wasn't asked. In the hasty perusal of seven or eight questions, it can be such a simple matter to mix up the contents of Questions Three, Five and Six on your first pass, get to Question Eight, dismiss it instantly in cold horror and then race back to answer Question Five, which now seems your likeliest bet – but, instead of reading it over, because you think you know what it says, you start answering it instead; and if you don't read all the questions through before you leave the exam hall, you won't realise that the

Question Five you've spent three-quarters of an hour answering exists nowhere but in your head – which you are now at liberty to smack in the usual manner at the post mortem.

A variation on the above, but also the immediate result of not reading the question right through and with care, is when a familiar word or phrase in a question fools you into thinking you know what the question is about. Before rational thinking returns, you're triggered into making an answer, the substance of which will, in very short order, depart from that which is required by the question.

In both of these mistaken activities, frenzy plays a significant role – a frenzy born of desperation based on the assumption that you are not in possession of the information requested, an assumption which may or may not be true, but one which you will regard as true until you calm down, stop emoting and start thinking. I appreciate that this is easier said than done under exam conditions, but there's no substitute for it.

The Secret Language of Examination Questions

Since the basic intention of exam questions is to give a little information and ask for a lot of information in return, the language and syntax used to achieve this purpose have to be very carefully handled. Questions have to be clear, specific, and succinct in the use of both individual words and phrases. Whatever their shape may be, good exam questions should quickly identify the subject of their enquiry and indicate the nature of your response. The vast majority of them do just that, and spending some time on looking at how they achieve these ends will be useful. We'll take three headings – Perspective, Individual Words and Phrases.

Perspective

In most professional examinations, the examiner's perspective is concerned with investigating how you handle information that underpins professional activity. In other words, the examiner wishes to discover whether you know relevant 'theory' and can link it pertinently with 'practice'. ('Theory' here is used to mean *any* information you might be expected to retain as part of your personal knowledge base.) Of course, it's expected that your identification and explanation of 'theory', your description of 'practice', and the relationships you demonstrate between the two are correct.

This perspective is sometimes very plain:

'Mrs Black, a 73-year-old woman, has suffered a Cerebral Vascular Accident which resulted in a right-sided hemiplegia.

(a) What difficulties might Mrs Black experience in resuming an independent life at home?
(b) Describe the elements of a nursing Care Plan aimed at restoring Mrs Black's independence to as high a level as possible.'

and sometimes a little more complicated:

'Discuss the possible uses of research activity in daily nursing practice.'

but always invites a response where specific information is handled in a reasoned and reasonable way. This application of 'Perspective', then, can be seen as setting the scene and the tone of exam questions, governing both the content and the means by which the enquiry is expressed.

Individual words

These can be divided into two general categories: Pavers and Pointers.
'Pavers' are words which indicate specific points about the information delivered in an exam question. For example:

'*Mr* Smith, a 48-year-old *carpenter* living on the *10th* floor of a *multi-storey* building with his *wife* and three *teenage* children, has recently been diagnosed as having lower motor neurone degeneration.'

While the last part of this sentence contains specific 'medical' data, this is prefaced by important items of information which 'pave' the way for a complete understanding of the eventual question – we know that we're talking about a married man with a young family, who is employed in skilled manual labour and lives in a high-rise block of flats, and *then* we learn a fact about him that has the capacity to affect his and his family's lives in a multiplicity of ways. The biographical data we've been given is likely to prove very important in making a response to the question. It can be seen that the inclusion of material like this goes beyond 'padding out' a question – the examiners have handed you some highly pertinent issues in Mr Smith's life which you must juggle appropriately in formulating your response. The idea behind it is sound: professional practice doesn't take place in a social vacuum, and neither should enquiries into the knowledge base of the person who will administer that practice.
Some 'pavers' arrive on their own, nestling quietly somewhere in the question:

'On being brought to the ward from Accident & Emergency in an *anxious* frame of mind, Mr Green's blood pressure is found to be . . . '

'During her *first* ever admission to hospital . . . '
'While undergoing a series of *invasive* diagnostic tests . . . '
' . . . and describe the nursing care required by Mr White in the 24 hour period following his operation.'

All of these serve to indicate a piece of information which you should know, but the last example, dealing with a time period, can be crucially important. Note the presence of every 'paver' and figure out how it will affect your response, but pay close and particular attention when *time* is mentioned in a question – it can set strict boundaries on the shape of your answer which you will be expected to be sharp enough to spot and abide by.

'Pointers' are words which are used to guide your answer in the direction desired by the examiners. Commonly used 'pointers' are:

– Describe
– Explain
– Discuss
– Compare
– Contrast
– Outline
– Identify
– Summarise
– State
– List

All of these, and others (see below), should be read and understood in conjunction with the information to which they relate, and heeded, because they tell you what the examiner wants you to do in collating and presenting your answer. So, if you're asked for a list, don't deliver a *Discussion*, even if it is about your pet subject. If you're asked to *Contrast* one thing with another, don't provide a response which contents itself with separate *Explanations* of these things. If you're asked to *Discuss* a topic, give it the full treatment, don't just *Summarise* it. And so on. Be as specifically responsive as you can, and look out for any 'qualifying' terms that might have something to say about the 'pointer':

'Describe *briefly* how nursing care might . . . '
'Give a *detailed* list of . . . '

and remember that while some 'pointers' may seem to require the same response, they are not synonyms for each other. There is a difference between *Describe* and *Explain*, where the second requires the demonstration of a greater degree of comprehension than the first. For example:

'*Describe* the clinical features of Thyrotoxicosis.'

as opposed to:

'*Explain* the clinical features of Thyrotoxicosis.'

and similar differences may be found between other 'pointers' when the context in which they are placed is considered:

'*Outline* the potential causes of pressure sore development in the patient who is bedfast.'

which calls for a list with brief details about each item;

'*Summarise* the nursing measures that may be taken to prevent the development of pressure sores in a patient who is bedfast.'

which calls for a combined identification and explanation of items and activities, given in a potted version.

Examiners sometimes depart from commonly used 'pointers' and substitute words and phrases which are close enough to the meaning of the original to be treated as synonymous in intent. For example, '*Give an account of*' for '*Explain*', and '*Detail the . . .*' for '*Describe the . . .*'.

Taking them together, and considering them in context, 'pavers', and 'pointers' provide you with a firm grip on what questions are all about. The only thing left to identify and explain is the way in which this context is constructed.

Phrases

Besides the grammatical nuts and bolts of stringing words together to make sentences and make sense, examiners will construct questions by including phrases which serve to 'fill out' the meanings and messages that will be presented. For example:

'Describe the specific nursing treatment of . . . '
'List the factors most commonly associated with . . . '
'Identify and discuss the main objectives of health education in . . . '

'In relation to . . . '
'State the most likely and immediate needs of . . . '

These types of phrases should be actively looked for in questions, since they also tend to circumscribe the nature and extent of your answer, besides helping you grasp and understand the enquiry itself.

Slightly different from these 'message amplifying' phrases, but used with the same intention of underscoring the meaning and purpose of an exam question is the 'notational' phrase or sentence, where an informative statement is made for you to consider in relation to a question. For example:

'In 1860, Florence Nightingale wrote that:

> "No man, not even a doctor,
> ever gives any other definition
> of what a nurse should be
> than this – 'devoted and
> obedient'. This definition
> would do just as well for a
> porter. It might even do for
> a horse."

Discuss this statement in relation to the development of organised nursing and its acceptance as a profession in society.'

'"Quality assurance in health care is
everybody's business." (McMahon, 1991)

Discuss the measures that may be taken to ensure that nursing care is of a consistently high quality.'

While these statements give you a 'slant' on the subject, their presentation is usually kept as neutrally worded as possible, to allow you greater freedom in presenting reasoned views in a balanced discussion.

Examination questions are carefully set so as to deliver instructions for making an answer, and always strive to encourage a clarity of understanding and help you achieve a clarity of purpose in making your response. That's the examiner's contribution. Yours is to read the resulting questions with enough care and attention so that you do yourself justice in the exam and hit the targets set for you.

The Language of Examination Answers

Each answer that you provide in an examination will be carefully sifted through by at least one examiner who, we can rightly assume, possesses an expertise in the subject being examined: this requires that your answers should be written in as careful and precise a manner as you can achieve. We can also assume that every examiner is a human being: this requires you to bear in mind that as cool and impartial as every examiner is, the human being inside has to be communicated with in certain ways, ones which encourage the appropriate reception and understanding of your written work. The following suggestions should help you do both

Write plainly

Exam answers are not the place for making literary flourishes in grandiloquent prose. Write in a straightforward style and as simply as you can. Marks are awarded for correct responses, not creative brilliance. The first and most fundamental requirement of your answers is that the examiner should be able to read and understand them without straining, without having to fish around for meaning, without having to piece together whatever it was you were trying to say and didn't bother to express properly.

Stick to the point

Say what you want to say, but say it briefly and without straying from the matter at hand.

Respond with reasoning

Demonstrate your knowledge and make sure you display it appropriately – logically, with organisation and order. Shuffling facts and figures and ideas around in your answers isn't enough, you have to show that your ability to comprehend and use information is at least equal to your ability in recalling that information. In other words, dredging a slew of data from your memory and jotting it down in whatever shape it appears when it first floats into your mind won't serve you as well as the response which is clearly the result of reasoning. Present your answers with data in the correct order, move sequentially from one point to another as the nature of the material dictates. Use titles, headings, sections and sub-sections – illustrate the meanings and messages you wish to convey and emphasise your grasp and understanding of the information by demonstrating comprehension and the ability to reason.

The only way to do this is to think about your answers before you write them down. Please don't be offended at such an obvious piece of advice. Sitting down to an exam can detach you from your normal habits, especially when you're crammed to the brim with recent learning – reasoned thought can lag a long way behind data regurgitation when you turn over that paper and the clock starts ticking.

Lastly, and more as an aside here, since these topics are covered elsewhere in this book, avoid waffle and avoid making baseless claims for half-remembered or just invented material. It's not possible for you to so antagonise an examiner that your answer script will be marked unfairly – there are too many checks and balances built into professional examination systems for that to happen. But: why annoy an examiner in the first place? Experienced examiners are long sensitised to waffle and fabrication – steer clear of them, even if you're sorely tempted.

So, the exam has started, you know what's required of you, you've read and understood every question, you're determined to turn in answers which will be pertinent, lucid and as well-written as you can manage. Which answers will these be, and what order do you write them in – 'best' first and 'worst' last, with another two shoved in between, so that you have time to muster every possible mark out of them in a decreasing order which is in direct proportion to your level of knowledge? Or will you tackle your 'worst' answer first and get the half-baked, barely understood material out of the way, so you can concentrate on working up to your 'best' answer, which will be a model of its kind? And does all of this really matter? Yes, and for two good reasons – the first of which is time, and the second is the consumption of energy. Both are important, and both will be used up by you in ways which are dependent on the methods by which you select questions to answer and the order in which you write those answers.

Selection and writing order

Selecting the questions you will answer is an easy task. You pick the ones you know most about, without fooling yourself about which ones might be 'easier' to get marks from. The yardstick for choice is a ruthless appraisal of personal knowledge. There are no tricks in professional examinations.

The writing order is less straightforward but is also based on what you know about the topic covered in each question: your best and most complete answer first, then the 'next best' and so on. Once you've decided what this order will be, note it down.

Now, subtract 15 minutes from the time that's left in the exam and divide this figure by the number of questions you have to answer, and use this last figure as a guide to the time you allow yourself for answering each question. For example:

If the exam lasts 2½ hours, and you've spent 7 minutes reading the instructions and questions and making your selection, you have 143 minutes left in the exam. Taking 15 minutes from this gives you 128 minutes which, if you have four questions to answer, affords you 32 minutes for each of them.

This doesn't sound like a lot, but it should be enough for writing your responses. Remember that you still have this 'extra' 15 minutes in reserve, and you can apportion this out carefully as you write each answer. A very full answer can be given a few extra minutes to complete – but don't use up all of this time margin just in writing; some of it must be used for reading over and correcting each answer *as it is finished*.

So, with an individual 'time target' in mind, begin writing and turn out the best answer first. Make it accurate, reasoned and reasonable, organise it well and construct it with logic. When it's done, read it over and correct any omissions or mistakes. Now, check the time; if you're over or under your target, note this but pass on to your next question and write it with the original time target in mind. When this second answer is completed, right down to the reading-over, check your time again: if you've used up more time than you intended, divide what time remains equally between the last two questions; if you've got 'extra' time in hand stick to the original time targets for each of the questions left.

With your 'old' or 'new' time target in mind, answer the third question. Again, read it over, check the time, and then begin your final answer. Here, we can pause for a few 'what ifs?'.

- What if you've written screeds of material for the first three questions and there's only 15 minutes left for the fourth?

Don't panic, this just means that you've given the first three a very fair shake, which included reviewing and revising them, an activity the value of which can hardly be stressed enough. With these remaining 15 minutes you can still make a sensible, ordered answer. It might not be complete, but then it was the one you were least confident about in the first place. Go straight on and do your best, but leave time enough to read it through at least once so you can spot and correct any obvious mistakes.

- What if you find you've got 45 minutes in hand to answer the last question?

Good. Give it as much time as it takes for you to drain yourself dry of the most reasoned answer you can provide, and then spend the remaining time going back over your other answers, in a reverse 'best' order, making sure you've done them full justice.

Besides the intention to plan and organise your efforts in the exam, time targets and 'best' to 'least best' ordering also help to direct your energy into appropriate channels. Completing a good first response can settle you down tremendously without making too many demands of you. It can also raise your confidence level and help dispel concentration-wasting anxiety, and as a useful side-benefit when it happens, the immediate experience of writing a good, ordered and reasoned first answer can help you to 'pattern' the rest of your answers. The time targets are set to prevent you switching off your attention from the fact that the exam will end *soon*. When you first sit down in an examination $2\frac{1}{2}$ hours can seem like forever, but once you're into your answers, time can race by and the end of the exam can take you by surprise, with a question barely begun or completely untouched. This is not a position you want to find yourself in – marks are distributed across the total number of expected responses for an exam – no one will rejig the hundred marks just because you're an answer short.

Frameworks for Answers

Constructing an exam answer as you go along filling up the pages of an answer booklet *is* possible, and varying degrees of success may be attendant upon it. But this two-stage activity – the trawling of information from memory and its immediate transferral to paper – isn't always productive of good, reasoned responses. The insertion of an intermediate stage – thinking – can be very useful. The act of thinking and the use of memory should precede writing, even in exams.

Memory aids and recall

The contents of exam questions are in themselves stimuli for the recall of pertinent material, so chew them over and extract as much information from them as you can, using it to prompt your memory. Take each question item ('sectioned' questions are a great help in this) and jot down what it brings to mind that is relevant and useful to you. Add the contents of any appropriate mnemonics or other 'pre-packaged' memory aids that will help. Do this quickly, and don't worry about how it looks. Make it as complete as you can, then read through it. The likelihood is that more items of data will occur to you – add these – and that some items will be mistaken or irrelevant – delete these.

Making an outline

Use these jotted notes to make an outline of your answers *as they will appear in their final form*. Arrange the material in 'skeleton' form, paying particular heed to any appropriate *order* and *sequence* that should be imposed on the information. While the accuracy of your data is a priority they must also be presented in context, so consider these skeleton notes as a whole and satisfy yourself that they make sense – make sure they include sufficient detail to clarify the meaning of your information.

Using an outline

Read the question over once again, then read your outline through piece by piece and write your answer. Refer to your outline for guidance and 'flesh' out the skeleton notes as required. If more items of information occur to you as you write, note these in the outline first before committing them to a place in your answer. When you've finished, check that all information has been transferred from your outline, then go on to read your answer through, scrutinising it for its own merits.

Now, dispose of your outline and any other scrap notes that have been included in your answer booklet by drawing diagonal lines through them. You don't want them mistakenly included for assessment by the examiner.

It won't have escaped your notice that every activity I've recommended here suggest that these exams should be dealt with in bite-size chunks. I firmly believe that this is a good way of going about the whole business, and reduces exams to a series of logical and manageable steps which are well within your personal capacity. Exams can be worrying enough to put you off your stride, so the more organised you are in meeting their demands, the more *systematic* your response is to them, the more opportunities you create for handling them appropriately and well.

MULTIPLE CHOICE QUESTIONS (MCQs)

MCQs, or 'Objective Testing', formats can be used by examiners to investigate your learning, usually as a supplement to other types of assessment. A simple example of a Multiple Choice Question is given below:

1:   *Which of the following statements is true?*
     (a)   The Subclavius is a muscle inserted in the clavicle.
     (b)   The Subclavius is a small secretory organ in the neck.

    (c)   The Subclavius is a large vein situated in the upper chest.

    (d)   The Subclavius is the ligament attaching the clavicle to the sternum.

and from this you would be expected to indicate your response, which is often required on a separate sheet of paper – for example:

    1:    (a)   T [ ] F [ ]
             (b)   T [ ] F [ ]
             (c)   T [ ] F [ ]
             (d)   T [ ] F [ ]

so that you must tick or 'shade in' an answer to every part of the question.

This all looks straightforward enough, and with a bit of care and attention, it certainly can be. However, MCQ format exams can make special demands on you, and must be treated with caution and respect. I say this advisedly, because sometimes the relief learners feel at knowing an examination is by MCQ rather than essay questions leads them up the garden path: it's seen as an 'easy' option. It isn't. A thoughtful, well-prepared set of MCQs can illuminate the furthest reaches of your ignorance quicker and better than almost any other form of assessment.

The point is that MCQs can cover a very great deal of ground in testing your basic grasp of a subject – from the fundamental acquisition of knowledge to the ability to analyse and interpret information. A common misconception about these examinations is that they can some-how be fudged by learners making wild guesses about the material presented. However, if you stop to consider this for a moment, what kind of luck would you need to have in order to correctly guess at enough right answers to pass the exam? Believing that a sprint through an MCQ paper making stabs in the dark will help you to pass is naïve in the extreme. Like any other type of exam, this one must be thought about and prepared for. And the essence of that preparation can be summed up in one word – recognition.

Recognition

Now, before you go on to read this next bit, please make sure you've read, noted and inwardly digested the cautionary passage above. Take it to heart.

With that said, and listened to, here's the good news – if you've made the effort to get to know and understand the course material that will be examined in an MCQ format, these exams can be a godsend. They ask you to make your responses with regard to small information 'sets' which act as prompts to your memory. Essentially, for the learner who is well prepared, the substance of each MCQ is a memory aid, which is designed to trigger your recognition of the material and supply the required response.

Naturally, these responses cannot be plucked wholesale from the air, and you must also handle the information presented to you; but with a good knowledge base, and regular practice in the interpretation and analysis of that knowledge, MCQs cease to be a matter for chance, and you can face them with confidence. So make your preparations for MCQ exams as carefully as you would for any others. Read the course material, write about it, discuss it with experts and peers, think about it regularly, sort it out and consider it at length. Handle the information as exhaustively and comprehensively as you can. We'll take that last descriptor and explore it a little further.

Your knowledge base must be as comprehensive as you can make it, because MCQ exams embody the belief that while *depth* of learning is important, so is *breadth*. Not just in the sense that your knowledge base must be wide – it must also be demonstrated that you possess a coherent knowledge base, one that you have good access to, are comfortable with, and can use sensibly and logically. In this perspective, comprehensiveness becomes the touchstone of MCQs, and therefore the key issue for how you will achieve the correct preparation that will underpin your recognition of material in the examination.

Make extra efforts to chase and acquire every last little scrap of information you need to know. If there's a part of the course material you've been avoiding, bone up on it now. MCQs can crawl into the smallest spaces of a curriculum and sit there, witholding marks you might desperately need. And could have got, with a bit more work, a couple of hours more reading and discussion – *anything* that would have prompted your recognition enough to allow you to dredge up the right response.

Don't rely on guesswork and magic thinking for MCQs. With the right preparation, they can permit you to accumulate a very tidy bundle of marks, which will do you no harm when it comes to summative assessment time.

MCQ Formats

The shape of these questions can differ. Some, like the example already given, make (seemingly) straightforward enquiries:

2:   Which of the following statements is true?

but remember that *all* information needs to be interpreted, it needs to be thought about and considered, you need to extract the correct meaning. From the question sentence above, for instance, does it require you to identify just *one* 'true' statement for the list of alternatives you would be given? Or, reading it another way, is *every* 'true' statement to be identified as such? Assuming, of course, that the given alternatives do actually contain statements that can be agreed upon as being 'true'. They might all be 'true'. They might all be 'false'. The only way you can tell for sure that your interpretation of the sentence is correct is if you read the *whole* question carefully, and use your knowledge to analyse all the information available. You see what I'm getting at here – an MCQ does not solely consist of the first little introductory sentence or two. Don't fixate on what you've 'understood' the question to be *until* you've read and considered every part of it in relation to the rest. The yardstick for use here is your knowledge, which should help inform your understanding of the question if you give yourself time to bring it into play.

Fair enough, a language expert might suggest that a rewording of questions and a little rejigging of grammatical perspectives might be in order for people who set these papers, but that's not your problem. The response is up to you, so make sure you have properly read the question and set it into an appropriate context in your learning. *That's* your starting point.

Some MCQs go further than declaring a specific query in their opening sentence. You can be given a short paragraph or two setting out a situation and giving you data which you may *or may not* need in order to make responses to various questions. For example:

> John Smith is a 23-year-old man admitted to your ward for an emergency appendicectomy. He tells you he is experiencing considerable pain and requests analgesia. He appears to be rather distracted and confused.
>
> Later, after he has gone to Theatre, you check through his belongings and discover a quantity of what you believe to be illegal drugs – just as a woman appears who claims to be Mrs Smith and demands that all of her husband's property be handed over to her immediately.

A lengthy string of question 'sets' can be based on this 'scenario' which attempt to elicit responses to various enquiries. Some may appear quite simple:

> 3: Which of the following features are normally associated with appendicitis?

    (a) Pyrexia
    (b) Headache
    (c) Confusion
    (d) Abdominal pain

and may be so. Although the vagueness of 'normally associated with', 'confusion' and 'abdominal pain' can serve to distract you here, remember that you can't rely on question shapes to always be models of clarity. More of this later.

Other questions in the set can depart suddenly from the 'Case Study' type of enquiry, like the one below, and throw you off-balance a little. Where the viewpoint of questions in a series changes, be ready for it and spend a little extra time composing your thoughts before answering. Bear in mind that the data you've been given in the 'scene-setting' should be seen as a trigger – not a signpost. Don't run in the first direction that occurs to you. Think about it.

    4:   In the UK, a written record of patient's consent must be obtained before:
        (a) An operation requiring general anaesthesia
        (b) Any nursing procedure involving a minor
        (c) Any surgical intervention
        (d) Administering drugs by intramuscular injection

MCQs can range over large amounts of territory in one connected sequence. It pays to stay awake and aware and remain cautious. Stay attentive and quiz your knowledge base thoroughly before committing yourself to a response. Make sure that your recognition of material accurately reflects the substance of the enquiry.

Whatever format you have to deal with, and there are more than I have described here, they all function on the same basic premise – that you should be able to use your learning appropriately to discriminate between 'true' and 'false' information and to discern and correctly identify how related pieces of information are linked. To achieve these activities, you have to know what you're talking about; there's no substitute.

The timing of your responses to MCQ exam papers is as important as it is in other exam settings. The only difference here is that MCQ formats are often accorded shorter response times. No matter – the same rules of leaving yourself time to check your answers still apply, to review them for accuracy and completeness and to ensure that you've done everything required of you. You may find that in working through the paper, you have very little time in which to check it over. If this is the case, use it to scan for *misplaced* ticks or whatever indications the paper requires as an answer: make sure you've ticked or shaded-in or circled the answer you intended.

Don't, in the final few seconds of the exam, race your way through your answers with a pencil in one hand and an eraser in the other, ready to make frenzied corrections to responses that seemed right at the time and now look hopelessly wrong. If your first answer was the result of reasoned thinking and some consideration, it's best to leave it well alone and trust your first judgment.

Similarly, as the moments tick away in MCQ exams, it can be irresistibly tempting to provide responses to those questions you couldn't get a grip on earlier and left blank. Now, listen carefully; I'm not saying categorically you must never guess at an anwer: if there are no penalties for mistakes, where's the harm? A few judicious guesses might in fact do you some good; but I don't recommend it – if you do your level best to answer honestly, the result you obtain will be a reasonable measurement of your learning in that area, and will help inform your own assessment of your knowledge base.

Besides which, not all MCQ exams are without penalties for incorrect answers. The dreaded instrument of *Negative Marking* is sometimes used in MCQ formats. The idea is simple – you get a mark for a right answer, and a mark is subtracted for a wrong answer. Simple, but deadly.

If you find yourself confronted with such an exam, you *must* limit your answers to those which you know are correct, or believe wholeheartedly to be correct. If you're *not* sure, leave the question alone; there are no penalties for not making an answer. This might result in a scanty response – so be it. Guessing at answers in a paper with negative marking is a certain route to disaster. I did it on two occasions and learned the hard way. Luckily for me, the resit paper set essay questions and I salvaged a pass. Don't be as stupid as I was. Don't guess; you have no room to manoeuvre with negative marking. Stay safe.

Lastly, we have to touch again on an issue that has been raised before – the apparent carelessness with which some exam questions are put together. I won't go over old ground here – MCQs bring some *extra* twists to the snaky messages of 'poor' exam questions.

1. MCQs should be brief and precise. The first is usually achieved, the second can be a difficult nut to crack. Teachers will take great pains to ensure that all terminology is exact and appropriate . . . and then apparently forget to apply the same effort to the rest of the material. The resulting question can look extremely ambiguous to a reader.

The example given above for the 'case study' question demonstrates this:

'Which of the following features are normally associated with . . . ' where we can pick out and (mis)interpret a few messages that serve to obscure the 'true' meaning of the sentence. For instance – a reader might hit on one message and fix on it:

(a) '*which* of the following features *are* normally associated with . . . '
(b) 'Which of the following *features* are normally associated with . . . '
(c) 'Which of the following features are *normally* associated with . . . '

and get into all sorts of brain-wracking anxieties about whether:

(a) means *more than one alternative is correct*.
(b) 'features' implies *clinical* features *diagnostic* of appendicitis, or is a shorter way of saying symptoms and clinical signs.
(c) the use of the word 'normally' is somehow especially significant and should be taken as a warning about the answer.

Whatever it is about any question that produces ambiguity, all you can do is to reduce it as much as possible by grasping the meaning of the question as a whole. Read it carefully to define the logical approach; don't waste time on getting annoyed.

2. The alternatives from which you must choose your response(s) in MCQs are all intended to 'look right', so that the winnowing out of the correct answer(s) demonstrates learning, not guesswork. However, sometimes, finding salient differences between alternatives can be a hard task when the resemblance between them is extremely close. So close, in fact, that you may think it's unfair. Just bear in mind that contriving these questions is a tricky business, and then look for any telltale clues in the question statement that might help; the decision as to which alternative to choose can be simplified if you find *qualifying* words which serve to narrow down your choice. For example:

'Which of the following is *always* found in . . . '

You still have to investigate your knowledge base for a response, but you can be more confident it will be the right one.

More clues can be found in statements which specifically mention factors which have the capacity to bring out or influence *change* in some way. For example, in a question about a certain disease, the *stage* of a pathological process might be referred to, and this could be very significant. Or even the passage of time – look for phrases like '24 hours later', '3 days after his operation, Mr Black experienced . . . '. They might help your understanding.

EXERCISES

1. From a collection of 'internal' and 'external' exam papers presented over the past three years, select at least a dozen sample questions covering as many different topics as possible. Now:

   (a) Rewrite each question by paraphrasing as much of the contents as possible – *including* any technical terms – and then try to summarise the meaning of the enquiry represented by the questions, for example:

      'In this question about the possible practical applications of health promotion by nurses, I need to discuss these in relation to both hospital and community-based care.'

   (b) Discuss your interpretation of these questions with a course teacher. If you seem to have missed some important points, ask for guidance.

2. Take four examples of these questions, on different topics, and make up a mock exam paper. Pick two questions about which you feel you might make a good response, and two which you think might give you problems. Set up a situation which mimics the conditions under which you will take an important exam, and then make every effort to answer the questions as best you can. Remember:

   Selection & Writing Order
   Time Targets
   Recall & Outlines

   Submit the results to a teacher and ask for *comments*, not *marks*. You want to know how appropriate the structure and contents of your answers are, in relation to the enquiries posed in the questions. Knowing how well you've constructed your responses is what matters to you here, not whether you would have passed this mock exam. Remember who chose the questions.

3. Whatever feedback you get from Exercise 2, take each question in turn and put together a specimen 'model' answer for each of them, referring to as many authoritative sources of information as required in order to ensure complete accuracy and sufficient detail. Make notes as you go and use these to create 'model' outlines for each answer.

   Submit both outlines and answers to a teacher for comments. Pay very close attention to the feedback you receive. Now compare these 'models' with your 'exam' outlines and answers, and try to highlight the differences between them, noting especially if you seem to display any obvious 'deficiencies' in handling the material under exam conditions – for example, providing insufficient detail or disordering appropriate sequences.

4. Obtain a Multiple Choice Question booklet on a relevant subject, or some exam papers set in this format and practise with them *under exam conditions*. Mark the results yourself with reference to authoritative texts. Do this marking in two ways: first, as a straightforward assignment of 1 mark for each correct answer; second, using 'negative' marking on the same material. Compare the results.

8 Cramming for examinations

The first thing to say about cramming is that it should be avoided. You do not *want* to put yourself into the position of having made so little preparation for any exam that you resort to cramming – it is *not* a sensible alternative to a reasonable programme of study and revision. So, if you're reading this chapter without an exam looming in the near future, be thankful.

However, if there *is* an exam just round the corner and you've finally admitted to yourself that without making *some* effort you're about to kiss success goodbye, read on.

EFFORT

You've avoided it long enough, you're going to have to do some work. But even now, human nature being what it is, you're maybe still mulling over some delaying tactics. For example:

(a) 'There isn't enough time left to make a difference anyway.' Enough time for what? If you're talking about grasping and understanding course material, you're right – it's too late for that; but if you've attended lectures, listened, learned and done some proportion of the course work, you might just have a basis for building some constructive effort. You're going to have to take the exam anyway, and scraping through by the skin of your teeth would be enough reward for *any* amount of work you have to do now.

(b) 'There's always the resit.' Is there? Maybe this *is* the resit; but even if it's your first bite at the cherry, it's not a rehearsal for something else – it's an exam. Get ready for this one as best you can. You don't actually want to fail.

These, and other statements in a similar vein, are excuses for putting off making an effort, and an excuse is a reason stuffed with lies. Stop finding excuses for why you can't or won't get started. Just start. And when you do, drop the guilt and regrets. Put all your energy into working.

First, consider this: *no one* expects you to display an intimate knowledge of every last particle of the contents of your course. What examiners *will* expect from you is a reasoned and reasonable response to enquiries into your knowledge base. What you're about to do now is to try and produce a limited set of those kind of responses.

Review the chapters in this book that deal with examination technique and then follow the guidelines below.

Time

Use every minute you can to study. Not just in your 'spare' time. *Create* as much study time as your circumstances allow. Squeeze the last drops of opportunity out of the time you have before the exam. If you've been the kind of person who made a full-blown ritual of studying – and then managed to put it off because things weren't 'just so' or you weren't in the mood – forget all that. Study anywhere and everywhere and do so constantly. If you're waiting for every circumstance to be perfect before you open a book, stop fooling yourself. It wastes time.

Revision

Whatever you've studied on the course must be revised, since you will have *some* knowledge of it and you cannot afford to ignore even a little learning. Gather all your course material together, put your notes in order and go over the ground you're familiar with. Acquiring new material comes next, but first consolidate what you know already, round it out and knock it into shape. This will provide you with a relatively manageable beginning to the rest of what you have to do.

Advice

If you're cramming because you haven't paid a great deal of attention, not only to your own studies, but to the course as a whole, *now* is the time to find out if teachers and peers have any comments to make about the forthcoming exams. You can't expect to beg and receive 'insider' knowledge, but you might be able to acquire a perspective on how sensible people are getting themselves ready – for example, are a number of people, or even one person whose views you respect, focusing on certain subjects or otherwise making a point of studying along certain avenues; is there any consensus of opinion among teachers and peers about identified 'important' topics that were highlighted on the course?

Essentially, what you're trying to do here is build up a profile of what other peoples' *expectations* of the exam might be; but you must treat anything you 'discover' with caution. Teachers are not in the habit of plainly telling learners the contents of exam papers before the event, and the groundswell of opinion among your peers as to what the exam will be about can be seriously mistaken. The point is that you may lack some part of the exam 'picture' which could help you and you should put yourself in the way of acquiring all information that could contribute to your understanding.

Be cautious. Do *not* commit all your efforts unadvisedly. It can be very easy when cramming to jump on to the first exam bandwagon that comes along and then to shut out other, more valuable, information. Be careful, and weigh up what you hear. Remember – this kind of activity isn't a substitute for studying. Do it quickly and get it out of the way.

Question-spotting as a *VERY* Inexact Science

Just about every learner tries to 'spot' questions that will be used in an exam. Some do it wisely, when their studying and revision is complete, in order to put some perspective on how subjects may be examined. Some do it for fun.

Others come to believe in it as a magic formula for passing exams. Crammers, for instance, who usually take the original shaky notion of spotting questions a dubious stage further and prepare a set number of 'specimen' answers, usually to meet the minimum requirements of the exam. This is a delusion.

Question-spotting has a place in the crammer's armoury, but it must be handled with great care and it should never, ever, be accorded blind faith. Try to spot questions by all means, but don't let the exercise grow until it bites chunks out of your studying time. *That's* the important activity; what follows can help you to study, it isn't meant to replace it.

1. Make a detailed list of all the course contents covered to date. Use subject headings *exactly* as they appear in the syllabus.
2. Gather together all of the relevant exam papers set within the last three years. Make sure you include resit papers and any 'class exam' papers that might have been used to prepare learners.

    From these papers, make a complete list of all subjects covered. If any topic crops up more than once, make a note of it.
3. Compare the contents of these two lists and see if you can identify a set of subjects which appear to be regularly examined. Note particu-

larly where any branch of a subject is reflected more than once in the exam papers.

4. Make a list of these identified 'exam subjects'. Now add it to the following:
   - Any subject newly introduced to the course
   - Any subject which has been suggested as 'important' by teachers and peers which is not already on the list
5. Take this list and review the exam papers again, making notes on:

   (a) Whether questions on any subject *appear* to be formulated in the same way at successive examinations
   (b) The 'amount' of the subject covered by questions in terms of extent and depth

Be very careful with your scrutiny of these questions. Don't just 'recognise' the contents and move on. Spend time discovering *how* the examiners might vary the approach they take in setting questions.

6. From the activity above, make out a full list of those subjects which seem to be highlighted by examiners, and note your best and most considered understanding of how examiners go about defining the response they expect. For example, one entry on your list might be:

Renal System: Mostly about Physiology. Anatomy questions rarely attract more than 10 per cent of marks.

   – Want to know how the kidneys regulate fluid balance in the body Marks usually 15 per cent of total for the question.
   – Covered at length on the course, cropped up in class exam.

However long or short this final list might be, it is only the *core* of a study programme that you can use. Don't concentrate on it to the exclusion of other subjects.

   Before going on to address the shape your exam answers might take, one final word of warning about question-spotting. Don't seduce yourself into believing a little pointed activity will supply you with the actual questions that will be used in the exam. Even if you do think you've spotted a pattern to questions – read around the subject identified as well and as widely as possible, there's no substitute for it. Now, having revised the material you already have to hand, it's time to begin cramming, to begin studying under pressure of time.

1. *Organisation* is your prime target. Whatever list you have of subjects

you will study, plan time for each of them and gather together all the material you will require – notes, books, journals. Do everything you can to ensure you won't waste precious time later by chasing down information you need.

2. *Set realistic objectives* for each subject in acquiring a breadth and depth of information about it. Use 'basic' texts for breadth in the most straightforward and simple format available, one that can be assimilated quickly. Create some depth to this information as soon as possible afterwards. If you can identify the expected 'depth' of knowledge expected about a subject from the final 'spotting' list, use this as a yardstick to guide your studies.

3. *Rehearse information* as soon as you acquire it and keep doing so right up to the exam. Read material again and again, make up mnemonics, recite it like poetry if you can. It's hard work, but in essence what you're trying to do here is to learn and revise at the same time; very little room is left for learning and understanding – the best you can hope for is to keep up the flow of information going in until some of it sticks.

4. *Don't give up* – stay positive, stick with it. If your programme begins to look too ambitious, change it, trim it, but don't dump it. If you're on the screaming edge and can't bear another minute, take a break. Then come back to the books and keep plugging away.

People who cram for exams sometimes rely very heavily on a little knowledge going a long way. Bolstered by a baseless confidence in their recent acquisition of a limited knowledge base that has still to solidify, they fall into one (or both) of two traps:

(a) The 'What I know is what you get' scenario; and
(b) The 'My specialist subject is Waffle' promise.

What I know is what you get

Here, the crammer glances at an exam question, recognises a subject heading and pours out every last scrap of material in their possession which seems even remotely relevant. Wildly expressed and disconnected torrents of barely understood data get plastered all over the paper in the vain hope that the examiner will choose salient facts from the mishmash and cobble together a pass mark – out of sympathy, perhaps.

Don't do it. Read the question. Make a reasoned and reasonable response. Your brain is supposed to be a cognitive instrument, not the unfiltered repository of everything that's ever come to your attention. You are required to sift through your knowledge base and produce only what's expected of you. If you can do that and produce a pertinent answer, however shockingly brief it looks to you, go ahead and do it.

Waffle is my specialist subject

Examiners are expert at spotting waffle, that woolly trademark of the learner who hasn't done a hand's turn in preparing for the exam.

Waffle comes in various forms, all intended to disguise ignorance: the grandiose phraseology used to spin out threadbare answers; the jargon-juggling which tries to conceal an inability to handle even the most basic concepts; the rephrasing of the same few lonely facts to fill another page or two. But you can't serve up drivel to an examiner and expect them to be fooled. If anything irritates an examiner, it's having to wade through streams of hand-knitted nonsense that transparently offer no other message than that you haven't a clue what you should be talking about. So, my strong advice to you is – don't waffle.

However, if you're really, really stuck, if you're doing your level best in an exam and answered all but one question and your only option is to submit an incomplete paper and certainly fail, or waffle and nearly certainly fail – then the waffle option might be your last resort. However, it will only 'work' in certain cases, where an exam format provides for 'informed opinion' answers to questions intended to explore your handling of information in a wide context.

If you *are* lucky enough to light on a question that seeks your opinion or asks you to discuss an issue suitably short on widely accepted 'truths', then you can go for it. Here are the rules, and you follow them at your own risk.

Rules for wafflers

1. Make your answer especially neat and tidy, no matter how heart-stoppingly trivial it might be. You want to create the impression of being an individual who, while they might be less than bright, at least possesses *some* values and is patently giving it their best shot. The appearance still will not make up for lack of substance, but every little helps.
2. Try to identify a theme or themes which you can stick to and upon which you can carefully hang your insubstantial patter. In other words *organise* your answer in some way. It might fall short of being entirely reasonable, but it should look as though it is a *reasoned* response. That might count in your favour.
3. Never imply any degree of validity for what you're saying. The

intentions of the wording used to define scientific veracity come rushing to your aid here. You are 'commenting' on a 'suggestion' that 'it might be argued' that what you're writing is not *absolute* tosh. You can state your opinions as plainly as you like but you must avoid defining them as being in any way 'true'.

4. Do your level best to avoid any 'depersonalisation' of your answer. You've been reduced to talking about you, so you might as well admit it in writing. Avoid the godlike overviews, which are usually accompanied by question-marks – as in: ' . . . and who are we to say whether that is right or wrong? Indeed, the sum of human experience, if it teaches us anything, rightly teaches us to ask ourselves "Am I not my brother's keeper"?'

    The examiner wants to know what *you* think, not some indeterminate segment of the entire population. Writing in the third person is one thing, acquiring a spurious omniscience is quite another. Keep in mind that it's you who is being asked questions, not the individual who's marking your paper.

5. Lastly, finish on the firmest ending you can manage. Don't fade out as though the last drop of mental energy had just been expended. Keep it as sharp as you can. Don't delude yourself into believing a half-finished last sentence will fool an examiner into thinking you might have gone on longer if you only had more time. You're using enough ploys already, don't use the one that tells examiners with excruciating clarity – 'I think I can fool you with this old chestnut.'

That's it for waffle, where just about the only certainty you have is that it might be sufficiently acceptable for an examiner to dole out a few marks as a reward. Where every mark counts towards the overall score, these few just might push you towards success. But nothing's guaranteed.

One final point about the whole business of cramming: whatever material you cram for an exam will in all likelihood, because you never really learned it in the first place, vanish like the drifting snow from your mind within a very short space of time. A few lonely mnemonics might remain, and some bits and pieces which you can quote like Shakespearian verse, but the rest will go. If you don't create a coherent knowledge base, you can't expect the crammer's simulacrum to be cohesive. It falls apart rapidy, and you will have to acquaint yourself with it all over again. In other words, you'll have to make twice the effort you needed to make in the first place.

Once again, as I noted at the beginning of this chapter; if you're just reading through this without an exam hovering in the near distance, don't become a crammer. Don't fail to plan your studies, or you'll end up behaving as though you're planning to fail your exams.

9 Teaching in a peer group

A good many courses these days require learners to participate in peer group teaching exercises, where each member of the group is expected to prepare a talk on a particular subject and then 'present' it to everyone else. I will say immediately here that I know of no richer or more valuable learning experience than this. I also know that immensely worthwhile though teaching your peers might be to you, it also tends to generate remarkably similar states of fear among learners of every level of experience and education. The main reason isn't hard to guess: teaching your peers can offer you an unrivalled opportunity for making a complete prat of yourself. I know this for a fact, because I was that prat. I once delivered a peer group presentation of such astounding badness that it engendered a state of complete bewilderment in my listeners. When it came to 'question time', the depth and quality of silence in the room was so tangible it could have been folded up and used for a blanket.

I don't want this to happen to you. *You* don't want this to happen to you. Nor will it, not if you prepare for your presentation properly and follow a few straightforward guidelines.

MEETING COURSE REQUIREMENTS

Peer group teaching, like any other structured activity in your learning, is intended to provide you with a stimulus to learn. Worthy 'side benefits' are gained from it, but the basic idea is used to demonstrate to you that learning can have a two-fold purpose for professionals – you can learn both for your own benefit and in order that others may learn from you.

Embedded within that notion is the unifying principle for this requirement on your course – how well do you acquire and use relevant information? There is no hidden agenda here; if an assessment is to be made on your presentation, it will be pointed at the ways in which you handle the acquisition and transmission of information.

As always, first make certain of the subject assigned to you, or select from given alternatives a topic which suits and interests you. Be especially careful here, if you have a choice to make, of going for the high-faluting topic in order to dazzle and amaze. Stepping in front of your peers can be a big enough step by itself without compounding it by a giant leap into unknown learning territory.

Make sure you have a crystal-clear appreciation of the format your talk is to take. It might be that the only parameter placed on it is that of time. Whether it's five minutes, ten or twenty, find it out. Usually, the guidelines you will be given for these preparations offer you suggestions rather than make demands of what you must do. Check it all out with care anyway – for example, must you prepare and circulate a 'handout' to the group? do you have to use an overhead projector and acetates? must the group be 'arranged' formally or informally?

One important factor here is to discover whether you will be expected to prepare a report on your presentation. If so, is it to be in note form just detailing the contents of your talk and submitted before the event, or will it be prepared afterwards, to include your reflections on what you've learned from the experience?

Benefits

You *are* expected to benefit from this exercise. It wasn't just dreamed up by teachers to make you uncomfortable. As you read and learn the material you will need to know, the fact that the outcome of this activity is to present it for digestion by others causes you to 'order' your learning behaviour in certain ways that are different from the norm. First, knowing that you're going to have to teach it to others is a stimulus to your activity in itself; it's a very useful way of concentrating your attention. Second, while 'ordinary' learning can produce a well-organised knowledge base in the individual, the form imposed by the requirement of learning in order to teach offers us a ready-made system of organisation; just as you wouldn't tell a joke by supplying the punchline first, teaching others demands that the material is clearly presented in a logical order. Third, you are much more likely to realise the need to firmly grasp and truly understand the material – you will after all be standing up and talking about it in front of other people. 'Knock-on' effects are also expected to benefit you, and the consolidation of knowledge in your own mind by explaining it to others is the prime gain here. Others include the opportunity for you to act on feedback you receive from your listeners, whether stemming from questions about the material or a general evaluation of how clear and informative the presentation appeared. Last, these presentations can serve to boost your confidence as a learner – there is a great satisfaction to be derived from knowing you can helpfully inform other people from your own knowledge base.

We'll take this issue of confidence to explore the greatest obstacle you might face in making your presentation – Fear.

From the vague flutterings of a few butterflies in the stomach to the more florid symptoms of hot faces, trembling hands and a desperate inability to stop a dry tongue from cleaving to the roof of the mouth, we've all experienced the various sensations of fear and apprehension. It's natural, it's the human thing to do when faced with situations which threaten or embarrass us. But we can take a cooler look at this: nobody actually is about to threaten you. What does that leave us with, but embarrassment? We'll say this plainly – it can be very embarrassing to stand up in front of your friends and make like a teacher.

And? So? Are you going to be the only one that's embarrassed when the presentations are done? Will yours be the only one neck upon which will be etched the rosy bas-relief of a negative self-esteem? No. By far the majority of your peers will be dreading the whole business, so you're in good company. Just accept that being nervous and on edge is par for the course for these occasions. If your hands shake a bit and you drop something, pick it up. If you're working from prompt cards and you lose your place and dry up, find it again and carry on. If your mouth is dry, that's what glasses of water are for. Never get angry with yourself at displaying signs of nervousness, don't be upset with yourself at feeling apprehensive. All the things you might believe will result from a shaky presentation – derision and abject humiliation – will not occur. For two reasons – first, because the people whom you fear will mock you are perfectly well aware that you will be a member of their 'audience', and second, because you're going to go into your presentation extremely well-prepared.

Plans and Preparations

Get your material gathered first and learn it well, because the 'shape' of it – how you will present it later – is secondary to how well you know it. This needs to be pointed out because it's all too easy in these situations to concentrate on the mechanics of the presentation rather than the content. Get into the material and soak it up.

When you've done this, you will be much better able to select and order the information you want to organise into your presentation. The first rule in this selection is the obvious one. Choose material that is salient to your topic. That sounds so simple, but you must be extremely selective and align your choices unequivocal ly with what you need to impart to your listeners. You might find that one item or another lends itself to the development of interesting little side-issues, not exactly germane to the topic but . . . throw them out. Be rigorous. The second rule is to order your selections in a logical sequence, and make absolutely no assumptions about what your listeners might already 'know' about your topic. They might know a fair amount, they might know nothing. If the stream of information you will present is to make sense, there should be no gaps in the progression from one point to another.

Third, make the material fit the time available for its presentation. Now, you've started the whole exercise with the knowledge that you only have a certain amount of time to talk about your subject. Don't forget that. Incorporate your material into a written 'speech', fitting everything into a discourse that you feel comfortable about delivering. Write it out as near to your natural way of speaking as you can. Now read it aloud and time how long it takes to say. If it falls far short of the allotted time, two things might be wrong: (a) you need to build in more relevant information, either as new material or as a more 'in-depth' discussion of what's already there, or (b) you're gabbling. Work out which it is and correct it. Remember that if you're not usually a fairly slow and deliberate speaker, you'll probably need to reduce your talking speed from a normal 'conversational' rate. If, on the other hand, you're grossly over the time allowed, you have to consider where you'll prune the material. The likelihood is that you've crammed it full of data which can't be explained in the time at your disposal.

The important point to remember here is the obvious one – you have a set time in which to impart a certain amount of information: when you stand up before people in order to do so, you enter a special type of communications 'arena'. While you and your listeners are face to face, the normal 'give and take' of conversation will be missing. The pool of information you have at your disposal has to be transmitted in a reasonably coherent one-way stream from you to your 'audience'. This requires you to be fully aware of what you're saying and have the confidence to say it clearly, which, in this case, can be achieved by rehearsal. Writing your 'talk' out in full and saying it over and over again will not only allow you to time it properly, but will also acquaint you with the habit of hearing yourself speak the material aloud. We'll come back to how you do that speaking a little later.

Facilities and Equipment

Where is your talk to take place – in a small, informal 'discussion' room with easy chairs? Or in a lecture area, with rows of benches and all the other paraphernalia of chalkboards and spotlights? Or somewhere in between? Do you have any choice in the matter? You might have, even if this is not plainly stated by your teacher. Find out which it is, especially if you have some say in the matter, and for good reason; the contents of your talk will influence the way in which it is presented to some degree, but the environment in which it is to be presented can often be the major deciding factor in creating the final format. Sitting cheek by jowl with your audience encourages small-scale, 'intimate' presentations. Standing on a lecture theatre dais puts a wholly different character on the business.

Once you know where the presentation is to be made, you can consider the venue and the content of your talk *together* and come to some conclusions about how you intend to 'do' the presentation. The appraisal and selection of presentation methods is made simpler for you if you concentrate on choosing a 'style' of presentation and teaching aids which will clarify and strengthen the messages contained in the information you wish to convey.

Style

You might think the matter of 'style' in making a presentation is a bit frivolous, but if you consider it for a moment in light of how you've been subjected to various teaching styles over the years, you'll appreciate just how important the manner of your behaviour in delivering a talk can be. These few guidelines will help you in deciding how your presentation 'style' might be arrived at.

Speak clearly, plainly and loudly enough to be heard

Few things are more irritating to an audience than having to strain to hear a speaker. After only a very short time, no matter how interesting or valuable the content of the material might be, if it can't be heard, people start withdrawing their attention. If you are naturally a quiet speaker, or suspect you're a mumbler, raise the pitch of your voice a little and enunciate more clearly. Practise this when you're 'declaiming' your talk. Better still if you can manage to arrange it, deliver your presentation, in the selected environment, to a critical friend who sits as far from you as any member of your audience will on the day. Your aim is to be heard without shouting, for every word to be clear.

A good many people who make 'poor' presentations speak as though every word is bring wrung out of them by force. Lack of confidence is the prime cause here, but this can be, and should be, avoided; if the material is well-chosen, sound and informative – what more is needed in order to make a *good* presentation other than a clear, straightforward delivery? The main ingredient of which is *plain* speaking.

If you speak up and out, then you will be heard. If you speak plainly, then you will be listened to. Besides unavoidable 'technical' terms, use ordinary, everyday language to get your message across. You know from experience how easy it is to get lost in the convoluted presentations some teachers make, where it seems that every second word requires a dictionary to define it. Keeping your talk within easy reach of your audience is the biggest benefit you can confer, and plain speech will do that.

A very special word of caution: it can be seductively easy to stand up and trot out a specious conglomeration of seldom-heard and rarely used terminology, and hope by so doing to give your presentation that patina of expert learning aimed at convincing listeners you're a genius. Don't do it. Leading an audience to believe you're knowledgeable is not what you're about here, and it's all too simple a matter for them to decide on the evidence that you're not a genius, but a fraud. You're there to convey messages that will inform their understanding of the material. That's it; and it's too important for game-playing. Keep it simple, keep it plain.

Behave as naturally as you can

A good start to this is to rehearse your presentation and work through any 'stage fright' you may experience. Go through any actions as well as the words; deliver the talk standing up if that's what you'll be doing on the day, work from any 'prompt' cards you wish to use. In other words, practise your behaviour.

The point is that delivering a presentation can seem a highly artificial way of behaving when you experience it for the first time. It can feel uncomfortable and strange, both of which are properties of the *newness* of the occasion, and which you can offset by practice. You're working towards feeling comfortable with your presentation: it needn't be word- or action-perfect, just familiar. So long as you get yourself used to the demands made on you by the occasion, and prepare for it, you'll come across well.

Beware of tricks, jokes and anecdotes

For three good reasons. First, an audience has to be very tolerant indeed not to mind having some 'trick' played on it, even if it is well-intentioned and introduced to highlight some point or other. Concealing a piece of information until you produce it with a 'hey presto' flourish and make everything clear is not advisable, nor is asking for audience responses to some 'question' that invites people to make fools of themselves because of ignorance. Whatever, keep nothing up your sleeve. Treat listeners with respect. Remember that they might have enough on their plate following you through the material as it is; they may prove extremely loth to spend any more effort on paying attention to you after they realise you've been messing them about.

Second, 'jokes' in a presentation are a minefield. Whether you think you're a comedian or not, a reasonably formal presentation performed as part of a course assessment is not the venue of choice to find out for sure. Your purpose is to inform, not amuse. If that sounds too rigid, consider this: what happens if the joke falls flat? How will you feel then – is it liable to distract you? Of course it is. Or what happens if half of your listeners laugh and the other half don't – does that mean 50 per cent of them aren't paying attention or they just don't find you funny? And even if everyone laughs, how quickly can they be expected to refocus their attention on the business at hand – because they're not there to hear you tell jokes, are they?

The problem with jokes is that they can produce expectations in your listeners that don't serve the purpose of your presentation very well at all. An informal tone can be given to presentations by well-chosen pleasantries handled by an experienced speaker who can keep everything germane to what's at hand. As a learner, you can achieve much the same atmosphere by being yourself and making no demands of your audience other than to listen to what you're saying.

Traditionally, jokes in any speech are supposed to relax listeners and make them more receptive; but your audience will already be receptive, if only because each of them will make their own presentation to you and wish not to offend you by a display of inattention. The person who might benefit most by the use of jokes as 'ice-breakers' is *you* as the person most in need of being put at their ease. In considering how risky jokes can be, accomplishing a sense of ease is best pursued by knowing and understanding the material.

Third and last, anecdotes devour valuable time and are rarely, if ever, as informative as a few well-chosen phrases that stick to the theme of your message. Most people who work anecdotes in to a presentation are usually making a point about themselves rather than the material, and are usually content with entertaining rather than informing. You're really not in a position to experiment with colouring your material with amusing or grim tales. Be satisfied with the plain message.

Now, whatever I have to say about tricks, jokes and anecdotes and the multitude of problems they can bring in their wake for the novice presenter, you might still embroil yourself in using one or all of them to 'improve' your talk. If you're caught inextricably in the feverish excitement of doing so – please use just one of them, not all three; and if you must use one – tell a joke. One joke, and leave it until the very end.

Teaching aids   Any and all teaching aids you might use in your presentation each have the same purpose – to clarify the messages you will present. This clarification may take several forms, but none is intended to replace your oral delivery. That is, your explanation of information, its description and discussion, comes first in order of importance and attention to detail. Any other medium of communication you use should be intended to supplement, not supplant, your talk. The greatest source of information your audience will have lies in hearing what you say. So, the best way to select teaching aids is first to decide whether any information you will present would benefit by being selectively emphasised in some way. You can do this by using a few rules of thumb:

(a) Will you be presenting a stream of facts and figures that your listeners should pay particular attention to?
(b) Is there any essential information that you feel would be better grasped by your listeners if they were given a visual prompt in understanding it?
(c) Are you presenting any information that may prove to be entirely novel to your listeners?
(d) Are you linking information in unusual ways in your talk, perhaps by suggesting 'sequences' to data which your listeners may find unusual?

Asking these and similar questions of yourself, scrutinise the contents of your presentation with care. Fundamentally, you're asking 'What needs to be clarified?'.

It might be that you're as satisfied as you can be that your messages need no other support in transmission than you can give them by simply stressing various sections of your talk. If that's how you find it, fine. You don't always have to use teaching aids; but beware of being over-familiar with the material and assuming it's clearer in the hearing than it actually is. Try it out on an unbiased listener and check if they've grasped all the main messages you wish to convey. And bear in mind, even if a trial presentation gets good reports, some course teachers want and expect you to use teaching aids. Always comply with their recommendations.

If you've quizzed your material well, you should find that the identification of points that should be emphasised, highlighted in some way, is fairly straightforward. Write these out as concisely as you can while maintaining sense and keeping them in the order in which they will arise in your talk. Now think about the teaching aids that are available to you and consider how each of them may be used for your purpose. You will probably have access to at least a chalkboard, an A1 'Flipchart' and an overhead projector, so we'll consider these in some detail.

Chalkboard   Familiar and easy to use. Helpful if you remember to write large and keep information to an absolute minimum. Chalkboards can be very handy for the novice presenter: when you stand up to talk, you can go straight to the board and use it with very little fuss. However, it has to be said that chalkboards have fallen greatly from general favour, possibly for much the same reason that would deter your own use of them – the very act of using them in writing or drawing diagrams often serves to distract attention when it should be most concentrated. If material needs to be written down, a format that can be prepared beforehand and referred to *as the material is discussed* can be of much more help to you.

If you decide to use a chalkboard, use it sparingly. Stick to 'headings' and one or two bits of information. Don't try anything complicated.

A1 'Flipchart'   These can be used in situations where you have a small- to medium-sized audience for whom the chart is easily visible. Prepare sheets beforehand if you possibly can. Use broad-nibbed dark ink pens and write large. Keep text simple and keep it to a minimum.

If you want to use the chart as you go through your talk, make sure you have two or three spare pens to hand. Use the top half of four pages rather than every square inch of two. Your message will be much clearer. Be careful when turning pages – they can be very unwieldy and I've yet to use a flipchart that didn't attempt to unload its entire contents at the presenter's first unwary handling of it. Practise with your flipchart until you properly get the hang of it; this includes the ability to write horizontally while standing upright before it.

Overhead projectors   These machines, which cast light through transparent 'acetate' sheets to throw an image onto a screen, are at once the most useful and most over-used teaching aids available. They are useful because they allow you to present written information in an easily visible form; they are over-used because (a) the simplest and most easily comprehensible information is sometimes fed through them in a tedious succession of wasted acetates by people who feel somehow incomplete if they can't fiddle with a projector and screen; and (b) there is an art and science to preparing OHP acetates which an unusually large section of the teaching population seem to have no inclination to acquire.

If you decide to use acetates and an OHP, either because your material lends itself well to being summarised into related informational 'bits' or because you wish to emphasise some material for a large audience for whom an OHP image would provide the best visibility, or even because you're just desperate to use the thing, a few guidelines are in order.

Get to know how the machine works   Practise with it. Where is it plugged in? How is it switched on and off? How do you focus the image? Is a spare light source bulb available, and how easily is it changed? How is the screen positioned – can you adjust it to suit you? All of this is so basic and yet so vital. Fiddling with an OHP during a presentation because you haven't learned where the 'on' switch is needn't be disastrous, but it can knock a sizeable hole in your confidence. Don't let it happen.

The same thing applies to the acetate sheets. If you've never used these before, try them out. Static electricity can build up between these sheets and separating them can be a tricky business. If they come with thin or tissue backing paper, discard this and back them between preparation and use with ordinary white typing paper of at least 80 gsm weight. Peeling recalcitrant acetates apart during a presentation is not recommended as a fun pastime.

Remember always to use the correct type of marker pens on acetates. Anything else will smudge. Special erasers are available for correcting mistakes – be careful when you do erase something on an acetate and always try the sheet on the machine before you do the presentation – sometimes 'erased' material will still show up faintly.

Writing your acetates   Prepare all the information you want to appear on acetates on paper first so that you can plan it out with care. Be strict with yourself and limit both the number of acetates used and the amount of information that each of them contains. Shuffling through a sheaf of acetates like a Mississippi card-sharp is a recipe for a disjointed presentation. If every sheet is crammed with data into the bargain you're going to have to be a miracle worker to hold people's attention. Keep them few in number and sparingly written-on. Acetates are the perfect medium for well-chosen and clearly detailed diagrams and other graphics, so don't neglect these if they will serve your purposes.

As a rough guide, leave the lower third of each acetate blank. Unless a great deal of open space lies between the screen and your audience, some part of the viewing surface will be obscured, and with it any of your material projected there. Similarly, leave reasonable margins at the top and sides: 3 cm or so should be enough.

Write boldly on your sheets, and print clearly. Don't cramp letters or words together, separate them out, underline them, use asterisks to draw attention to especially important points. Overhead projection doesn't cure illegible, poorly presented script, it just magnifies it. Take some time over the appearance of what you write – but please try to avoid the following:

Samplers of penmanship. Some people, when writing for the 'big screen', go overboard to make every acetate a work of art. Curlicues and pot hooks are scattered everywhere and good, plain messages are lost in a welter of distracting nonsense. The simplest possible form of writing should be used, and that's *printing*.

The rainbow acetate. Just because your acetate pen set offers you half-a-dozen colours to choose from, it doesn't mean you're in any way forced to use them. Stick to black or dark blue. If you feel that you must use another colour or burst, try red; and use it just to underline or for asterisks.

Remember you're always striving for clarity here, always stressing plain messages in the strongest possible way.

One last 'don't' here, which I won't link with those two above, because it's a very personal one – don't use cartoons on acetates to get messages across. Even if it doesn't look amateurish to the point of embarrassment, it will probably alienate a high proportion of your audience. People can get very prickly about how they are taught anything, and sometimes cartoons are taken as a sign that they're being 'talked down to' by the presenter. Your reception as a cartoonist might not be that problematic, but I can tell you that few other actions you take in your presentation can backfire so immediately and with such unwanted results as flipping a cartoon onto an OHP when the audience expected to be informed. If you've never made a peer group presentation or sat through someone else's efforts, you're perhaps wondering why I've introduced this notion of cartoons at all. Be patient, you'll see them soon enough; and if the urge to draw some witty, telling little cartoon on to an acetate ever threatens to overwhelm you personally, resist it. Please.

Putting it all together When you know how the machine works, and your brief set of lucid acetates is ready, go and practise your presentation. As you go through your talk, use each acetate in turn. When you are as convinced as you'll ever be that the material is straight in your head and you can manage the equipment, number your acetates in the correct order. Now practise again, and aim to get each acetate on and off the OHP smartly and without fuss – ingrain it as a habit, because you're aiming to let nothing distract you from speaking up and speaking out and speaking clearly. Never lose sight of that. The OHP and acetates are only adjuncts to your communication with your listeners.

'Handout' Texts for the Group

Even if the course requirements don't demand that you prepare some kind of 'handout' text for the group, think seriously about putting one together anyway. Written information that can be used as a reference during the presentation and afterwards can bolster your message in a very helpful way. In a more mercenary vein, a thoughtful, informative handout text can do you no harm when it comes to course assessment of your presentation.

A few simple guidelines for preparing these texts are sufficient:

1. They should be informative, but brief. Treat them as a vehicle for providing a reasonably detailed synopsis of your presentation. Make sure they include all the relevant material you will discuss. Taking headings from your outline notes is a good way to put a text together, with short paragraphs underneath, covering the vital points you will raise.
2. Include a full Reference List/Bibliography for the material you use. If you found any particular source of information especially helpful, say so. Draw up these lists with the same care you would take in preparing any research-based piece.
3. Wherever possible, prepare them in typescript.

As an added bonus for your group, you might want to consider using a little ploy that can be very helpful to you: arrange the text on your handout so that space is left on each page for note-taking. Starting a presentation by informing the group that you've not only prepared a handout text for them but you've also made sure that taking notes will be made easier can warm people up immediately. You've already got their attention, and it's positive.

So now you're at the stage where you know and understand your material and you've selected any teaching aids you might use. You've rehearsed your presentation as though it were a speech and you've practised 'slotting-in' the appropriate use of acetates, or whatever. So what's left? Holding it all together and making sense in the face of your peers is what's left.

Very few of us, as novice public speakers, are sufficiently self-possessed to permit us the use of certain faculties we normally take for granted – such as remembering what we were going to say next; very, very few of us have an instinctive understanding of how to teach others. But we can learn to do both, or at least present an acceptable simulation until the real skills arrive through practice.

First, how do you remember to say everything you intended to say? I've already suggested that writing out and rehearsing your talk aloud will help – and it does, enormously. To put a final touch on getting through all the material you have, prepare a series of prompt cards in two stages.

Stage one   Write out on successive cards every important point you wish to raise in the course of your talk, add as much detail as you wish to include. When you're happy with the original rehearsals of your presentation, try doing the same thing just with these cards. If you find there are 'gaps' creeping in, alter the cards in some way to remind you to deal with the material in full – for example, use a highlighter pen to shade passages you've missed. Practise again until you can deliver your talk completely.

Stage two   Now reduce the information on the first card set to a series of 'target information' points – *not just headings*. Briefly note words and phrases in small clusters of information, write the minimum that will remind you of everything you want to say. Don't let the number of cards grow unwieldy – so long as your talk is covered then the fewer cards the better. Number them clearly.

Next, practise your talk with these cards, and take careful note of the last point made from each card as it is used in sequence. These 'last points' are your *cues* for where you are in your presentation. If you 'work from' your cards during the actual talk before a group, you will only have to glance down to check your cues to see if you're ready to move on. This comes with practice and relies on your rehearsal of the material; you develop your recall of the sequence of the delivery of your information, and still have the fail-safe of having accurate 'prompts' to hand.

It's worth noting here an issue that will already have become perfectly obvious; I keep stressing the requirement to practise your presentation, from the first writing out of what you will say to the use of these prompt cards. Don't be dismayed at all this rehearsal; remember that these presentations are often very brief. Practice needn't be onerous and too time-consuming, but it will give you all the opportunities you require to embed the material in your memory. If the process appears mechanistic, it is intended to permit you not to sound mechanistic when you do your presentation. When you stand up to speak, everything you need to know will be firmly in your grasp and this is the best position you can be in to do well.

Presentation Format and Behaviour

First, you tell them what you're going to tell them, then you tell them, then you tell them what you've told them. In other words: a brief introduction, the main messages and a brief summary. Simple, direct, appropriate. Waste no time on lengthy preambles before you start your talk. Waste no time in winding up when the material is covered.

In the in-between bits, try the following.

Speak naturally

Don't orate, recite or declaim. Keep a normal tone in your voice and all the usual inflexions of everyday speech. Pretend you're speaking to just one person because, if you think about it, that's exactly what you're doing. There is a group of individuals before you, not a group mind. Give them an easy access to your material by talking about it in as natural a way as you can manage.

Look at your listeners

This can be a little difficult to do at first. So do it first – look each one of them right in the eye in turn and keep doing it. Maintain eye contact as much as you can. Most of them will be looking at you for most of the time anyway, so why not look back? What else can you do – look away? Eye contact helps to engage and retain people's attention and you *want* that, you want them to focus on you and what you're saying. Scatter your gaze among them, look them in the eye briefly and pass on to the next one.

Be enthusiastic

Be positive about your presentation and bring enthusiasm to it. Brighten your face and smile, convey an attitude of personal *interest* in what you're saying. Mind the body language; don't hunch up and hide behind the projector or desk, don't squeeze up against the nearest wall as though you wished you could pass through it and make your escape. Step in front of them and stay there – *be* there and be animated. Groups can be very sensitive to a presenter's mood and can have the uncanny knack of feeding their perceptions straight back to you. You want positive feedback, you want to produce interest and enthusiasm among your listeners, so do something about generating it. Give them a 'model' attitude to focus on. Try it, you'll be pleasantly surprised.

Most presentations of the kind you will undertake should have a brief 'question time' built in to them, not for prolonged discussions, but for the elucidation of any points you raise. The best way to be prepared for this is to know the material well. Remember, though, that you couldn't possibly answer every question that might be asked. Be content with that knowledge. If you're asked a question to which you don't know the answer, say so; then do your best to point the person in the right direction for finding out the answer for themselves. Nobody will expect you to have an encyclopaedic knowledge, but they will expect an honest response.

Inviting questions and some discussion of your material is helpful for both you and your listeners. You can check up with each other if the messages have been transmitted and received appropriately. When your presentation is over, you might have no other thought in your head but to step off the stage and sit down. Pause for a moment – you put a lot of effort into making a good presentation, but how well did it come across? What can you learn from that? When the whole business is over and done with, your peers might informally tell you it was 'fine' or 'interesting' or 'much better than anyone else's'. All well and good, but you want to know a little more than that. At the end of your presentation, you can afford to give a brief time to eliciting responses to the following questions:

1. Was the material clearly presented?
2. Did anyone learn anything from it?

which you do not preface with the killer query: 'Are there any questions then?' Give them encouragement to speak. Ask instead something such as 'Is there any particular point you want me to go over again?' or 'Is there anything I didn't make quite clear?' What you're trying to do here is use the contents of your presentation as a mirror, held up to reflect your performance by pointing it at the material. People feel less constrained at asking questions if it seems less personal to do so, especially if they wish to make what might appear to be a 'negative' comment.

So, while you seek to help your listeners learn, you're also minding your own learning. Naturally, a complete evaluation of your presentation, and by far the best informed, will be delivered by your teacher. Heed the feedback well.

Part of this evaluation may rest on your submission of a report that details the contents of your talk. If guidelines are available for you to follow in preparing it, then read them with care. It is very unlikely that you will be required to provide an 'essay'-type submission, complete in every detail, but they must be accurate and they must be a true representation of your talk. Keep the following in mind:

1. Be rigorous in sticking to the contents of your presentation; don't glitz it up with a fortnight's extra effort that didn't go into your talk.
2. Use all the material you presented. This should include a copy of any handout text you distributed and direct transcriptions of the contents of acetates or other visual aids.
3. Reference lists and Bibliographies should be compiled with due care and attention. If you have chosen to supply your peer group with a 'recommended reading' list, include this with the reasons why you selected the texts noted.

A final word. There are as many different ways of making presentations as you have the imagination to conjure up. What I've suggested here has the keynotes of good preparation and simplicity. If you decide to go for broke and attempt an Oscar-winning performance, remember that you still have to be well prepared, you still have to be knowledgeable and you still have to get the message across.

EXERCISES

There's no reason why you shouldn't have a go at doing piecemeal what a full-blown presentation will require of you as a complete performance. Try the following:

1. Select two topics for a presentation – one you know a good deal about and one to which you have only recently been introduced. Set yourself a five-minute 'reading time' limit for the finished article and then, without reference to *any* source material, write out a specimen 'talk' for each of them.

   Now check them over with care and cross out every phrase or passage that represents nothing more than a personal statement or opinion about each subject. Take whatever is left, which you might think of as your 'factual' material, go to the authoritative texts and find out if your 'facts' are anything of the kind. Cross out everything you misrepresented, either because it wasn't a fact or because you disordered the information in some way. The likelihood is that you will now be left with very little, not because you're stupid, but because you might not be used to combining information with the notion of presentation. Don't be disturbed if your 'best' subject fares in much the same way as your 'worst'. All you need is practice, which will define the requirements of your task.

Do the whole exercise over again, but this time, work from reference texts. When you've finished, sift through them for any repetitions and cross these out. Check for gaps in connections between one point and another – fill these in where they occur with brief statements. Now rewrite both until you're satisfied with them, and hand them over to a teacher for (preferably written) comments on how suitable they might be as material for a presentation.

Pay very close attention to any feedback you get. Discuss it with the teacher.

2. Arrange to have access to any teaching aids you might use in a presentation. It won't take you long to become familiar with them, so persuade someone to let you have fifteen minutes or so worth of practice. Write something on a flipchart (or chalkboard) and then go to the furthest reaches of the room – is it clear enough, can it be read with ease? Try out an OHP with a couple of acetates – how does the image look? Did you forget to remove the backing paper before you put them on the screen?

    You might find (I hope you don't) that some institutions are a little chary of releasing equipment for practice like this. Ask anyway; you don't have to apologise for trying to put a learning experience together. Point this out in the nicest possible way, and don't be offended if a teacher comes along to 'supervise' you. Just accept it as a nice gesture and carry on – you can always put their presence to good use and ask them questions.

3. From one of the talks you wrote out at the first exercise, try preparing an accompanying handout text. You're only working from five minutes' worth of material so it won't take long. Draft it until you think it fairly represents a synopsis of the 'presentation' and then have it read over by another learner at the same stage in the course as you. Ask them for feedback, based on whether it appears to be clear, concise and informative. Pay particular attention to any indication you receive that the reader 'got lost' anywhere in the text. Remedy any bare patches, bridge any possible gaps without the piece becoming too lengthy.

4. Practise speaking to an audience of your peers. This is easy advice to give and might prove impossible for you to take, but you can shape the exercise to suit you and your circumstances. For example, if you find yourself in a sizeable group, look at each of them in turn when

you speak. If you say something that invites a response and some don't make one – ask them what they think. The simplest statements can help you sort out an understanding of how you come across to other people. Try saying something such as, 'Did that make sense?' after you've said something.

I don't expect you to corral a group of friends and make them sit through a practise presentation, but you might be surprised at how amenable your peers could be to a suggestion that you act for each other as a 'support' group in preparing presentations. If they agree, you've just found yourself some listeners.

Index